Relationship-Driven
Classroom
Management

This book is dedicated to all the teachers who manage to capture the hearts and minds of their students without excuse, despite numerous obstacles put in their way.
To my son Julian. I hope I can practice what I preach.

Relationship-Driven Classroom Management

Strategies That Promote Student Motivation

John M. Vitto

CORWIN PRESS, INC.
A Sage Publications Company
Thousand Oaks, California

For information:

Corwin Press, Inc.
A Sage Publications Company
2455 Teller Road
Thousand Oaks, California 91320
www.corwinpress.com

Sage Publications Ltd.
6 Bonhill Street
London EC2A 4PU
United Kingdom

Sage Publications India Pvt. Ltd.
B-42, Panchsheel Enclave
Post Box 4109
New Delhi 110 017 India

Printed in the United States of America

Library of Congress Cataloging-in-Publication Data

Vitto, John M.
Relationship-driven classroom management:
strategies that promote student motivation / By John M. Vitto.
     p. cm.
Includes bibliographical references (p.   ) and index.
ISBN 978-0-7619-4677-9 (Cloth) — ISBN 978-0-7619-4678-6 (Paper)
   1. Classroom management. 2. Teacher-student relationships.
3. Motivation in education. I. Title.
LB3013 .V53 2003
371.102´4—dc21

                            2002154962

This book is printed on acid-free paper.

14 15   8

Acquisitions Editor:	Rachel Livsey
Editorial Assistant:	Phyllis Cappello
Production Editor:	Julia Parnell
Copyeditor:	Cheryl Duksta
Typesetter:	C&M Digitals (P) Ltd.
Indexer:	Sylvia Coates
Cover Designer:	Michael Dubowe
Production Artist:	Michelle Lee

Contents

Preface

Effective teachers have high expectations for their students and provide the necessary supports for their students to live up to these expectations in an environment of low threat. I have attempted to write this book in a way that would challenge teachers in a nonthreatening manner and also provide them with the supports needed to succeed.

WHOM IS THIS BOOK FOR?

This book is designed for teachers, administrators, and support staff who are interested in classroom management strategies that enhance teacher-student relationships. If you are looking for a classroom management book full of quick fixes, this might not be the book for you. If, on the other hand, you are interested in a classroom management book that focuses on prevention, enhancing teacher-student relationships, long-term behavior change, and resilience, then this is the book for you.

WHAT IS RELATIONSHIP-DRIVEN CLASSROOM MANAGEMENT?

The purpose of this book is to empower educators to use classroom management strategies that enhance relationships and social-emotional skills. These factors have tremendous power to increase academic performance and build resilience. The importance of positive teacher-student relationships is not new to educators; however, discipline and management styles that weaken these relationships abound. An overreliance on common discipline strategies such as reactive strategies, punishment, harsh comments, nagging, yelling, and power struggles, to name just a few, can hurt teacher-student relationships.

Although research has shown the importance of positive relationships, resilience, and social-emotional literacy in prevention and learning, it does not appear to have translated into classroom and schoolwide management practices. A relationship-driven classroom focuses on proactive and behavior management strategies that enhance teacher-student connections, promote social-emotional competency, and protect children from future risk.

The Importance of Relationship Building

The most significant difference between this approach to classroom management and most others is the high priority placed on preserving and enhancing the teacher-student relationship. While many approaches indicate the importance of building a positive relationship prior to intervening on a student's behavior, the relationship-driven approach views building the relationship as a most powerful intervention. We may not always realize how our classroom management strategies place a wedge between us and our students. Relationship-driven classroom management strategies strive to prevent and correct misbehavior without hurting the teacher-student relationship.

The Link Between
Behavior and Academic Success

Most teachers strive to maintain caring and positive relationships with their students. However, making this a priority can be difficult with the recent demand for higher state test scores and accountability. This book will provide evidence that the goals of higher test scores and positive relationships complement rather than conflict with one another.

Many classroom management resources ignore the connection between academic success and student behavior. Since classroom behavior is so closely tied with academic success and failure, the relationship-driven approach focuses on preventing misbehavior by implementing effective instructional strategies that enhance academic success and increase student motivation.

The Benefits of Social-Emotional Skills

This book is unique in its focus on behavioral and social-emotional skill building. Teaching behavior and social-emotional skills are just as important as academic skills and often need to be taught in a similar fashion. The relationship-driven approach focuses on teaching students appropriate behaviors and social skills rather than punishing students for inappropriate behavior. When students possess these skills, motivation and achievement increase, misbehavior decreases, relationships improve, and resilience is fostered.

Teacher Self-Evaluation

Another unique feature is that the relationship-driven approach asks teachers to examine or self-evaluate the discipline strategies in their toolbox to determine their long-term effectiveness and what impact they have on the teacher-student relationship. The reader will find numerous questions throughout this book and at the end of each chapter that are intended to facilitate teacher self-evaluation. Behavior change and motivation are stronger and more durable when the decision to change is based on self-evaluation rather than externally imposed by an authority figure. If the strategies you are currently using are working in more than just the short term and are preserving and enhancing your relationships with your students, by all means keep using them. If they are not effective or put distance between you and your students, consider trying some other strategies this approach offers.

In writing a book about teacher-student relationships and discipline, it is difficult to avoid using negative examples. I have tried to find a balance of negative and positive examples. Negative examples are included for learning purposes and should not be interpreted as blanket statements about teachers in general. Most teachers have the best intentions when they are dealing with students. This book is ultimately about being optimistic about the power of teachers to impact the present and the future quality of life of their students.

ORGANIZATION OF THE BOOK

The bulk of this book is essentially about preventing misbehavior rather than reacting to misbehavior. Chapters 1 through 7 cover prevention, resilience, teacher attributes, proactive strategies, relationship-building strategies, teaching and modeling of social-emotional skills, enhancing academic success, and student responsibility. Implementing these strategies will significantly reduce the amount of necessary reactive strategies. Reactive strategies are covered in Chapters 8 through 10. Topics in these chapters include effective consequences, strategies for difficult and resistant youth, and assessment of classroom management.

ACKNOWLEDGMENTS

I would like to thank the following people who made this project more successful:

Rachel Livsey, Acquisitions Editor at Corwin Press
Myra Vitto
Steve Vitto
My colleagues at Canfield Village Middle School
Patrice Loree
Judy Parsons
Michelle DeFabio
Patrice Loree

The contributions of the following reviewers are gratefully acknowledged:

Brenda Waugh
PAR Consulting Teacher
Resource Specialist
Newhall School District
Valencia, CA

Rosie O'Brien Vojtek
Principal
Ivy Drive School
Bristol, CT

Diane Holben
Curriculum and Academic
    Services Coordinator
    9–12
Saucon Valley High
    School
Hellertown, PA

Karen Harvey
Beginning Teacher Support and
    Assessment Program
    Coordinator (BTSA)
Santa Clarita Valley BTSA
    Consortium
Santa Clarita, CA

Catherine H. Payne
Principal
Gov. W. R. Farrington High School
Honolulu, HI

Ron D. Wahlen
Technology Facilitator
Wake County Public School System
Conn Global Communications
    Magnet
Raleigh, NC

Deborah Wilks
Third Grade Teacher
Riverside Cultural Arts and
    History Magnet School
Wichita, KS

Patricia Schwartz
Principal
Thomas Jefferson Middle School
Teaneck, NJ

Debra S. Preston, Ph.D.
Associate Professor and School
    Counseling Program
    Coordinator
University of North Carolina at
    Pembroke
Pembroke, NC

Dr. Patrick Akos
Assistant Professor
University of North Carolina
Chapel Hill, NC

Ellen Reller
Mathematics Teacher
Everett Middle School
San Francisco, CA

CORWIN PRESS

The Corwin Press logo—a raven striding across an open book—represents the happy union of courage and learning. We are a professional-level publisher of books and journals for K-12 educators, and we are committed to creating and providing resources that embody these qualities. Corwin's motto is "Success for All Learners."

About the Author

John M. Vitto is a parent, special educator, school psychologist, and author. He specializes in behavior management, prevention programs, solution-focused counseling, reality therapy, and conflict resolution. In addition to his work in schools, he has worked in two psychiatric hospitals and in private practice. John is an adjunct instructor at Mount Union College. He is a member of the National Association of School Psychologists, Council for Exceptional Children, and the American School Counseling Association. John has presented at state conferences on relationship building, conflict management, and the creation of optimal learning environments for students. He enjoys jazz music, movies, and exercising. Questions or comments can be directed to jmvitto@aol.com.

PART I

Preventive Strategies

CHAPTER ONE

Relationship-Driven Classroom Management and Resilience

"For the resilient youngster a special teacher was not just an instructor for academic skills, but also a confidante and positive model for personal identification."

—Werner and Smith (1989, p. 162)

CHAPTER OBJECTIVES

In this chapter the reader will learn:

- The definitions of resilience, risk factors, and internal and external protective factors
- Research on teacher-student relationships and resilience
- The importance of resilience and social-emotional skills in learning
- How teachers can develop student resilience
- The importance of resilience and relationships in violence prevention

UNDERSTANDING RESILIENCE

Most of us have heard stories of people who give teachers credit for having a great influence on their lives. Stories about teachers who encouraged students to improve, to overcome, and to be better than they believed they could be. Some people can even recount the exact assignment and the exact words or phrases that the teacher used that changed their lives. These stories are inspiring and reflect the impact teachers can have on the lives of their students. However, the influence of the individual teachers is lessened due to the time it takes for students to realize the impact a teacher had on them. Students usually do not attribute their success to their teacher until the students are long out of school. Most of the time teachers do not know which students they had a profound effect on. We tend to forget in our day-to-day dealings with students the powerful impact we can have on their lives.

Werner and Smith (1989) studied children with multiple risk factors (poverty, strained parental relationships, poor role models, etc.) for 40 years. They found that one out of three of these children developed into competent adults. They then studied the children who were able to succeed despite living with much stress and adversity and identified factors that were present in these successful children; these factors form the basis of resilience. Werner and Smith found, among other things, that these children often credited a favorite teacher who went beyond academics and became a mentor, confidant, and positive model for personal identification. This chapter is about the positive power of teachers to influence the quality of life of their students.

There is a large and growing body of evidence of the tremendous impact teachers can have on students' quality of life, including affecting whether students engage in harmful behaviors and affecting their emotional health and resilience (Resnick et al., 1997). How can teachers have such an impact? As we shall see, much of this research points to one critical factor in the classroom: positive and personal teacher-student relationships.

Most teachers want to connect with students. Time constraints, curricular demands, accountability, and testing pressures can interfere with the teachers' desire to have positive and personal relationships with students. In addition to these constraints, many discipline models operating in schools, especially those that rely heavily on punishment, hurt teacher-student relationships.

Unfortunately, many school reform initiatives focus on inadequate solutions, such as vouchers, increased testing and accountability, year-round schooling, harsher punishments, and zero-tolerance policies. These solutions are shortsighted and ignore critical factors such as the importance of positive teacher-student relationships and the development of social-emotional competencies and resilience. If we are going to have a working knowledge of resilience, we must first understand risk and protective factors.

Risk and Protective Factors

The goal of the relationship-driven classroom is not only to prevent student misbehavior in the short term but also to help students learn the skills that prevent the development of more serious personal and socially destructive behaviors. To prevent destructive behaviors such as violence, substance abuse, mental disorders, early pregnancy, and school dropout, we must strive to prevent the development of known precursors to them. These risk factors include, among others, poor self-control, early onset aggressive behavior, academic failure, social conflict, poor interpersonal skills, poverty, broken homes, and poor parental attachments. Although educators are unable to control many of these risk factors, we can gain an understanding of protective factors—how some children beat the odds and succeed despite serious adversity. If we understand protective factors, we can teach and nurture them in all students.

Protective factors are attributes or assets that when present protect the child from developing harmful, destructive, and ineffective behaviors. It may help to remember what protective factors are by viewing them as assets. Protective factors contribute to students' resilience. Researchers have isolated the critical protective factors by studying the lives of those children who overcame adversity, despite having many risk factors. Generally speaking, the more protective factors children possess, the more resilient they are said to be. Simply stated, a resilient child is one who "works well, plays well, loves well, and expects well" (Benard, 1995). Resilient individuals are able to manage and rise above adversity and stress in their lives. While it is necessary to strive to prevent risk factors, it may be more important to build protective factors or assets, so students are better able to cope with inevitable adversity. To do this, teachers must understand the distinction between external and internal protective factors.

Figure 1.1 Protective Factors of Resilience

External Protective Factors	Internal Protective Factors
Care and Support	**Social Skills**
➢ Close bonds	➢ Self-awareness
➢ Positive role models	➢ Empathy
➢ Support of friends	➢ Communication skills
	➢ Conflict resolution skills
Setting High Expectations	**Problem-Solving Skills**
➢ High expectations for all students	➢ Generation of alternate solutions
➢ Provide support necessary to achieve high expectations	➢ Abstract and flexible thought
Encouraging Meaningful Roles	**Self-Control**
➢ Valued for their contributions	➢ Delayed gratification
➢ Genuinely needed	➢ Mood regulation
➢ Given meaningful roles, responsibilities within the home and school	➢ Thought of consequences before action
	Self-Efficacy
	➢ Belief that they can have influence on own life
	➢ Belief that they can accomplish goals
	Optimism
	➢ Hope for better future
	➢ Goal directed/persistent
	➢ Nonnegative explanation of events

Internal and External Protective Factors

External protective factors are present outside the student and involve the family and school environment. High expectations, supportive and caring adults, and significant relationships are some examples of external protective factors. Internal protective factors, or social-emotional skills, are characteristics or attributes that the student possesses, such as self-control, relationship or social skills, problem-solving skills, optimism and hope for the future, and a sense of self-efficacy. Self-efficacy is the belief that one can accomplish a given task and that one possesses the power to exert some positive influence in one's life. The internal protective factors, or social-emotional skills, can be taught and are very similar to the components of emotional intelligence (Goleman, 1995). Figure 1.1 summarizes the internal and external protective factors. Throughout the rest of the book the term *social-emotional skills* will be used instead of internal protective factors.

Strengthening of social-emotional skills has been shown to reduce aggressive behavior and violence (Conduct Problems Prevention Research Group, 1999), mental disorders (Rutter, 1990), academic failure (Rathvon, 1999), chemical abuse and early pregnancy (Hayes, 1987), and delinquency (Michelson, 1987). Teaching and modeling these social-emotional skills are critical to a relationship-driven approach to classroom management. I address building these social-emotional skills in the classroom in Chapter 5. Resilience research can be summarized and simplified using three terms: *I have, I am,* and *I can,* such as in the following list (adapted from Grotberg, 1995):

I Have

- People in my life whom I trust and who love me, unconditionally and no matter what
- People who set limits on my behavior
- People who model how to do things right
- People who assist me when I am ill, in danger, or need to learn

I Am

- A likable and lovable person
- Respectful of myself and others
- Willing to accept responsibility for my own behavior
- Sure things will work out for me

I Can

- Talk to others when I am frightened or troubled
- Solve my problems
- Control my actions
- Find someone and ask for help

CAN TEACHERS FOSTER RESILIENCE?

Can teachers make an impact on these critical risk factors? Can they prevent future destructive behavior in their students? Ideally, both home and school work to develop protective factors for children. However, the school alone can make a significant impact on these protective factors. In fact, a recent underreported study of 12,118 adolescents by Resnick et al. (1997), titled "Protecting Adolescents From Harm," found that positive emotional connections to parents and teachers was the strongest protective factor. School connectedness was protective of every health-risk behavior (e.g., emotional health, suicidal thoughts and behaviors, violence, use of cigarettes, alcohol, and marijuana) except history of pregnancy. This study is significant to educators because these positive relationships and connections at school can prevent and protect adolescents from engaging in unhealthy behaviors in their future.

The study also found that having positive relationships with teachers was more important than class size, amount of teacher training, classroom rules, and school policy in protecting adolescents from destructive behaviors. Resnick et al. (1997) state, "Of the constellation of forces that influence adolescent health-risk behavior, the most fundamental are the social contexts in which adolescents are embedded; the family and school contexts are among the most critical" (p. 832). When students feel connected at school, they are less likely to engage in violence, drugs, alcohol, sex, or other harmful behaviors.

Positive teacher-student relationships are also cited as a significant contributor to academic achievement and motivation (Elias, 1997) and the prevention of dropout (Thurlow, Christenson, Sinclair, Evelo, & Thornton, 1995), bullying (Olweus, 1999), substance abuse (Resnick et al., 1997), and violence (Dwyer, Osher, & Warger, 1998). In summary, teachers can have a tremendous impact on resilience development in their students. This research is important and should lead us to seriously examine school and classroom practices. Are we doing everything we can to increase positive school relationships and to decrease student alienation? Do our school and classroom behavior management practices increase student connection or alienation?

WHOSE JOB IS IT?

One might argue that building relationships and resilience is not the role of teachers. They might argue that it is the role of the parents to develop these skills or that there is no time to teach these skills in addition to an overloaded curriculum. However, as families experience increasing amounts of turmoil and stress, schools take on additional responsibility for the well-being of children.

Is It Our Job to Help Students Be Effective Learners?

To be an efficient and effective learner certain social-emotional skills must be present. If students do not have positive peer relationships, feel supported and cared for, and possess problem-solving skills, beliefs that they can accomplish tasks, and self-control, they are not ready to be effective learners. The same social-emotional skills that foster resilience also are prerequisites for effective and optimal learning. In addition, when students possess well-developed social-emotional skills, they are less likely to misbehave.

Is It Our Job to Maximize Student Learning?

Learning, socialization, and emotions are not mutually exclusive but are interrelated and inseparable. If we neglect any of these components, we fail to tap into the full learning potential of the individual. The brain does not differentiate emotions from cognition, either anatomically or perceptually (Caine & Caine, 1994). Emotions either impede or enhance students' abilities to think and plan, to pursue training for a distant goal, and to solve problems (Goleman, 1995). We as educators need to fight the temptation to falsely separate academic and emotional competencies.

Is It Our Job to Prepare Students for the Workforce?

According to Goleman (1998), two out of every three of the abilities deemed necessary for effective performance in the workforce are social-emotional competencies. The skills often cited as most important are self-awareness, self-regulation, motivation, empathy, and social skills. In addition, the most frequent cause of job failure is lack of self-control and an inability to get along with others.

In an article titled "The Other Side of the Report Card" (Wang, Elias, Walberg, Weissberg, & Zins, 2000), the authors state, "Students who are actively engaged in class, who cooperate with their peers, who can resolve conflicts, who are motivated to complete their work, and who demonstrate initiative and leadership are more likely to succeed in school, and ultimately in life" (p. 1). The authors conclude that even though some parents and teachers are willing to give up a few test-score points for enhanced social-emotional competency, they do not have to because "recent research [shows] that enhancing children's social, emotional, ethical, and academic development are inseparable goals rather than competing priorities" (p. 3).

WHAT TEACHERS CAN DO TO FOSTER RESILIENCE

We know that resilience helps our students overcome adversity. Adversity occurs in everyday life for our students and comes in the form of friendship problems, divorce, illness, death, loss of job, moving, accidents, abuse, alcoholism, robberies, and so forth. Take a minute to consider the many adversities that your students experience. Do these adversities hinder your students' performance in school? You can foster resilience in your students to assist them in overcoming and coping with these adversities.

According to Benard (1995), teachers who promote resilience provide and model three protective factors: caring relationships, positive and high expectations, and opportunities to participate and contribute. I explain these factors in the following sections and show how they are integrated throughout the relationship-driven approach to classroom management.

Caring Relationships

Teachers convey love by communicating that they care, by listening, and by being compassionate, and they strive to establish personal and positive relationships that go beyond academics. The prevention and discipline strategies advocated throughout this book help to preserve and enhance these caring relationships. According to Benard (1995), the presence of at least one caring person provides support for healthy development and learning. This person is someone who conveys an attitude of compassion, provides unconditional regard, and does not take the behavior of their students personally because the person understands that the students are doing the best that they can given their circumstances. Students who experience caring relationships develop the belief "I am cared for and worthwhile." Strategies such as relationship building, classroom community building, social skills training, mentoring, advisory groups, and school within a school (for larger schools) help to ensure that all students are noticed and have at least one adult who knows them well. The degree of caring and support within a school or classroom is a powerful indicator of positive outcomes for youth.

Some classroom management practices may hinder the development of caring relationships. Classroom environments where there is a high degree of emotional or physical threat, ultimatums, and inconsistency hurt the development of trust, security, and respect, which are critical to the development of caring relationships. Students need appropriate consistency, structure, and behavior limits to develop resilience. Classroom management strategies that are inconsistent, harsh, coercive, and reactive, and those that lack empathy and understanding, hinder the development of resilience through caring relationships.

The importance of caring relationships in resilience is the basis of the entire relationship-driven approach to classroom management. Every prevention strategy and corrective strategy used in the classroom is chosen with caring relationships in mind.

Positive and High Expectations

Teachers who recognize students' strengths and interests and use these as starting points for learning bolster resilience. These teachers are able to help students recognize their strengths. For example, teachers could examine students more extensively for interests and strengths rather than for deficits. Once teachers are aware of the personal affinities and interests of the students, they can build in time daily or weekly for students to work in these areas. When students work within their areas of affinity and interest, high expectations are naturally set. When we allocate precious instructional time to a student's strengths and interests, rather than on remediating weaknesses, we send a powerful and affirming message to our students. Teacher expectations are often subtle but always powerful predictors of future outcomes. Teachers who maintain high expectations are able to challenge students to go beyond what they believe they can do. These teachers have a keen understanding of the negative and self-fulfilling effects of low expectations. Teachers set high expectations when they see something in students that the students may or may not see in themselves; they set low expectations when we see only labels, deficits, and past test scores.

Not only do they provide challenge and high expectations but also they provide the necessary supports to achieve these expectations. Teachers can do this by offering a varied curriculum and varied instructional formats (teacher directed, cooperative, small groups, etc.); valuing different cognitive styles or intelligences; allowing student participation, choice, and decision making on issues important to the classroom; and by matching the curriculum with the instructional level of individual students. In addition, teachers can provide more individualized instruction, guided practice, and support when necessary.

Teachers can assist students to be optimistic by helping them to not take adversity personally (i.e., blame themselves) and to see that their adversity is not permanent. Students who experience high expectations develop the belief "I am capable and competent."

In some classrooms references to negative behavior far outnumber acknowledgments of positive behavior. When negative statements and interactions outnumber positive interaction and statements, expectations may inadvertently be diminished. In addition, when adults hold grudges or frequently bring up past behavior, a discouraging message is sent to students. It is critical that teachers hold positive and high expectations not only for academics but for behavior as well. When we hold positive and high expectations for behavior, we send students the message that we believe they can choose more effective behaviors.

Effective teachers often have the unyielding belief that their students will learn better behaviors. These teachers use behavior management strategies that rely on positive feedback and effective praise to help maintain positive and high expectations. Positive classroom management strategies teach more effective behaviors and can assist in building resilience.

Opportunities to Participate and Contribute

Student resilience is enhanced when they have the opportunity to engage in meaningful roles and responsibilities in the classroom, school, and community. Teachers can assist students in this area by allowing them to express their opinions, use creative expression and imagination, work with and help others, give back to the community, and have a voice in curriculum planning and classroom rule development. Teachers who use cooperative learning, peer helping, cross-age mentoring, and community service facilitate resilience. These strategies create a connection or bond between the student and school, allow for practice with social skills, and decrease students' likelihood of engaging in destructive behaviors.

During the Christmas season the seventh-grade staff members at Canfield Village Middle School involve their students in a community service project. The students raise money, purchase and wrap gifts and food, and deliver these packages to needy families in the area. The most interesting aspect of this project is the noticeable lack of misbehavior and conflict. Students who normally were in trouble are engaged, and groups of students who normally are in conflict cooperate with each other.

One elementary teacher uses an interesting technique to increase opportunities to participate and contribute in meaningful ways. Each year her students pick a classroom charity. The students brainstorm the possible needs of the particular charity, and throughout the year the students engage in activities that target these needs. These strategies allow for meaningful contribution, which helps students feel like they are genuinely needed. In the past our students found these meaningful roles and contributions at home. At young ages they were needed to contribute with chores and responsibilities, or even financially, to the family. Most of our students no longer have these opportunities at home. When these opportunities are provided at school, they allow students to develop the belief "I am important and can contribute in meaningful ways."

Discipline procedures that prohibit students with behavior problems from participating and contributing hinder the development of resilience. Strategies that look for positive ways for all students—especially difficult students—to gain positive recognition and meaningful involvement help develop resilience. Students with behavior problems will often rise to the occasion if given an opportunity to help or contribute. This is especially true if it involves one of their strengths or interests. I remember one student with severe behavior problems who was an excellent "teacher's aide" in a class for children with developmental disabilities. The problematic behaviors normally present in his classes were virtually absent in this helping setting.

SCHOOLWIDE EFFORTS

While teachers can foster resilience in their classroom, a schoolwide effort is even more powerful. Positive schoolwide recognition for student accomplishments in social, behavioral, and artistic realms is one way to increase resilience. Asking your principal if you can send down a student or group of students for good behavior is another useful strategy. It can be very rewarding to students when principals call parents for good behavior. Creation of schoolwide social skills programs, rules, and expectations is another powerful strategy. In this strategy every classroom teaches and practices the same social or behavioral skill of the week or month. The assemblies, activities, and announcements for the entire school address this specific social skill. The entire school staff uses a common language for rules, expectations, and valued social skills. In situations where schoolwide programs are not feasible, a team of teachers can have a similar effect by focusing on specific rules, expectations, and social or character traits and use common language and strategy across all members of the team. A final strategy, schoolwide mentoring or advisory programs, helps to ensure that each student has the opportunity for at least one caring relationship.

I have briefly described several ways that we can foster resilience in students. When we build protective factors, all students are better equipped to handle adversity and resist destructive behavior. Why should we try to develop student resilience? One answer to this question is just because we are able to. Next I turn to the importance of resilience and relationships in violence prevention programs.

PREVENTING VIOLENCE

Resilience and relationship building also play a key role in violence prevention. Relationship-driven classroom management strategies preserve and enhance relationships and have the added benefit of helping to prevent violence. Schools that are safe are also effective learning environments. The recent cases of extreme violence in our schools have put the prevention of violence or safety at the forefront of all educational issues. Sadly, much of the focus goes to adding security guards, metal detectors, and security systems.

In a report titled *Early Warning, Timely Response: A Guide to Safe Schools* (Dwyer et al., 1998), the authors described 13 essential components of safe, well-functioning, and responsive schools. I chose to highlight the six following components because of their relevance to the theme of resilience in this chapter (although many of the 13 components are related to resilience): involve families in meaningful ways; focus on academic achievement; offer extended day programs for students; work in partnership with parents to promote shared values; have close ties to community support services, police, families, and churches; and support students in making the transitions to adult life and the workplace. Safe and responsive schools also do the following:

- *Emphasize positive relationships among students and staff.* Research shows that a positive relationship with an adult who is available to provide support when needed is one of the most critical factors in preventing student violence.

- *Treat students with equal respect.* A major source of conflict is perceived or real bias based on race, social class, physical appearance, and sexual orientation, either by staff or peers. Effective schools communicate in words and action that all children are valued and respected. They establish a climate that demonstrates care and a sense of community.

• *Make sure that opportunities exist for adults to spend quality/personal time with students.* Schools that allow time for relationship building send a strong caring and supportive message to the students. By making sure opportunities exist for bonding, student alienation is reduced.

• *Help students feel safe in expressing feelings, needs, and anxieties.* When students are encouraged to express feelings and concerns, they feel cared for and important. The opposite of this occurs when we discourage or punish emotional expression.

• *Teach students how to deal with feelings, manage anger, and resolve conflicts.* Safe schools teach and model positive strategies to deal with emotions and conflicts. Conflicts are seen as opportunities for growth not punishment. Teachers can model effective ways to manage emotions in the classroom.

• *Create ways for students to share their concerns.* Safe schools discuss safety issues openly and often. It has been well documented that peers are the most likely group to know in advance about potential school violence.

The majority of the components that the authors cite as critical to a well-functioning and safe school involve positive relationships with and among students and teaching students to express and deal with feelings. In your school or classroom are building positive relationships, encouraging students to express feelings, and teaching students how to manage feelings a significant and regular part of the student's education?

Interestingly, a common factor cited in more than 75% of the 37 cases of U.S. school shootings was the attacker telling someone beforehand that the shootings would occur (U.S. Secret Service Safe School Initiative, 2000). However, according to the report in almost no cases did the students seek out or tell any adults. This should tell us that we should be instructing all students in what to do if they hear such threats and give them a way to anonymously report them.

In addition, this finding hints that students may not seek advice or trust adults enough to go to them in these situations. A recent national survey by the Metropolitan Life Insurance Company (2000) of teens, parents, and teachers confirms this hypothesis: Lack of trust was the reason given most frequently by teens for not seeking teachers for advice or help. The report indicated that when students were asked whom they would seek help if feeling depressed, "friends" was listed by 77% of the teens, "family" by 63%, and "educators" by only 33%. Are we doing everything we can to foster student trust? Are we doing everything we can to keep the communication lines open between adults and students?

The U.S. Secret Service Safe School Initiative (2000) study also reported some interesting findings that relate to the topic of resilience and coping with adversity. In more than 75% of the incidents, the attackers had difficulty coping with a major change in a significant relationship or had experienced a personal failure prior to their school attack.

It seems that our money, time, and effort should go not toward physical security measures but toward enhancing and preserving relationships at school and giving students the coping skills to handle adversity and conflict. Social skills training, bullying prevention, and conflict resolution programs are excellent steps in this direction and will be discussed in Chapter 5.

SUMMARY OF MAIN POINTS

- Resilient students have certain protective factors both inside them and in their environment that help them to "work well, play well, love well, and expect well" (Benard, 1995).

- Internal protective factors or social-emotional skills, such as social skills, problem solving, self-efficacy, optimism, and self-control, can be taught and can help students be more effective learners and resist destructive behaviors.

- Teachers can foster resilience in their students by developing a caring and personal relationship with their students; by having positive and high expectations, with the necessary supports to live up to these expectations; and by providing opportunities for meaningful roles, participation, and contribution.

- We must go beyond external security measures such as cameras, metal detectors, guards, and zero-tolerance policies and focus on positive relationships and resilience if we are going to deter the threat of violence in our schools.

QUESTIONS FOR DISCUSSION AND SELF-EVALUATION

1. What are some ways you already increase resilience and social-emotional skills in your classroom or school?

2. What are some other ideas for increasing resilience for your school or classroom?

3. Does your school put more efforts toward identifying and remediating risk factors or building protective factors? Which is more important?

4. What can we do as educators to help prevent student alienation?

5. Does your schoolwide and classroom discipline practices help or hinder the resilience goals of caring relationships, positive and high expectations, and opportunities to participate and contribute?

ACTION PLAN

As a result of something that I learned in this chapter I plan to (be specific in your answer):

_____

_____

_____

RECOMMENDED RESOURCES

Benard, B. (1995). *Fostering resilience in children.* Urbana, IL: ERIC. (ERIC Document Reproduction No. EDO-PS-95-9.) Benard is a leading researcher on resilience and provides an excellent summary on resilience and schools.

Dwyer, K., Osher, D., & Warger, C. (1998). *Early warning, timely response.* Washington, DC: U.S. Department of Education. This document was created as a result of a U.S. Department of

Education commission on the study of school violence and contains numerous violence prevention ideas and programs.

Krovetz, M. L. (1999). *Fostering resiliency: Expecting all students to use their minds and hearts well.* Thousand Oaks, CA: Corwin. This book provides an excellent resource for educators who are interested in resilience. The author describes promising resilience projects in different school systems around the country and provides tools for assessing the resilience factors in your school.

U.S. Secret Service Safe School Initiative. (2000). *An interim report on the prevention of targeted violence in schools.* Washington, DC: Author. This report highlights the findings and implications for schools from the systematic study of the 37 school shootings and 41 attackers. The report calls for resources to be put toward prevention rather than law enforcement.

CHAPTER TWO

Attributes of Relationship-Driven Teachers

"It is difficult to give to our students, what we do not already possess."

—Author Unknown

CHAPTER OBJECTIVES

In this chapter the reader will learn:

- The personal attributes of an effective classroom manager
- The importance of practicing teacher and student self-evaluation
- The importance of self-evaluating beliefs about classroom management
- The common discipline myths and dangerous assumptions
- Strategies to maintain teacher enthusiasm

The purpose of this chapter is to look at the characteristics, beliefs, and working assumptions of teachers and their influence on classroom management practices. This chapter also contains strategies to maintain teacher well-being and enthusiasm. If we neglect our own well-being, it becomes difficult to maintain a positive attitude and be effective models for our students. In other words, it is difficult to give something to our students that we do not possess. Negative attitudes breed and lead to lowered expectations for ourselves and for our students.

PERSONAL ATTRIBUTES OF EFFECTIVE CLASSROOM MANAGERS

The personal qualities and beliefs of the teacher are critical variables in classroom climate, discipline, and resilience. The relationship-driven teacher strives to be an effective human being and has well-developed, or is developing, social-emotional skills (i.e., social skills, problem-solving skills, self-control, self-efficacy, and optimism). They understand that it is difficult to give and model what they do not possess. Teachers in relationship-driven classrooms model these skills and characteristics on a daily basis and to the best of their ability. Effective teachers have been found to have many personal traits in common, including the following examples adapted from the work of Walker and Shea (1991):

- They accept children for who they are rather than trying to make them something they are not. They accept children who are different without reservation.

- They are flexible and do not adhere rigidly to a particular intervention or lesson plan.

- They choose to work with children and know why they make the choice.

- As human beings, they are confident, realistic, and honest.

- They are willing to look at their own behavior critically, learn new skills, and make changes as necessary. They are not defensive about the manner in which they choose to deal with children in the classroom.

- They are willing to evaluate their own behavior and the classroom setting in addition to the child's behavior when analyzing problems.

The last two traits are central to the relationship-driven approach to classroom management. The greatest single attribute of relationship-driven teachers is the willingness and ability to take an honest and nondefensive look at the effectiveness of their own behavior, especially how their behavior influences the interactions that occur in the classroom. Effective teachers and classroom managers frequently examine what they are doing and change accordingly if necessary. They avoid repeating strategies that are not effective. In addition, they do not hold rigidly to the belief that it is only the child's responsibility to change: They understand that adults are usually more capable of change and that a small change by the teacher could lead to a positive change in student behavior.

In fact, many effective teachers carefully consider their own negative behaviors that detract from their overall effectiveness. A teacher once sought my opinion after a discipline interaction that took place in her classroom. A youngster had shouted out an inappropriate comment for the whole class to hear. The teacher calmly replied, "See me after class." According to the teacher, this technique had worked well in the past. So why did this teacher seek out a consultant? She wanted to know if there was a better way to handle the situation. She was concerned that the boy's anxiety about what would happen after class interfered with his learning and that he didn't learn anything the rest of the class period. This is an unusual concern since most teachers would enjoy letting the student "stew" awhile and not think about the student's ability to receive instruction. This teacher was able to take a deep and honest look at her own behavior in the classroom. This is called self-evaluation.

The least effective classroom managers, on the other hand, seem to deny the existence of the problem, become defensive, or assign blame to someone else (student, parent, principal, etc.). They do not seem to recognize, or in rare cases are unwilling to acknowledge, how their behavior influences the behavior of their students. Self-evaluation, or taking an honest look at the effectiveness of your own behavior, is the topic of the next section.

THE IMPORTANCE OF SELF-EVALUATION

It is critical for the classroom teacher to understand and practice self-evaluation. Self-evaluation is taking an honest and searching inner inventory of the effectiveness of your own actions, thoughts, and feelings (Wubbolding, 2000). In simple terms, it is judging the effectiveness of your own behaviors and thoughts. While this may seem like a simple concept, it is more complex when applied to life and to the classroom. All of us repeat behaviors that are not helping us get what we want. How often do we as adults engage in behaviors that are contrary to our goals? For example, we may procrastinate, overeat, fail to exercise, and nag our loved ones, even though we are aware that these behaviors are not usually effective. We are more accustomed to judging the behaviors of others rather than of ourselves.

Self-Evaluation Questions

Self-evaluation is facilitated by the use of questions, which help assess whether or not your behavior is effective in getting you what you want. We can also self-evaluate if what we want is realistic or helpful. Here are a few examples of self-evaluation questions that relate to classroom management:

- Does it help or hurt when I lose my temper with my class?

- Does it help when I fail to follow through with consequences?

- Does it help to take the behavior of my students personally?

- Is it helping my students to do their work when I lecture them about getting it done?

- Does it help or hurt to look at the situation in this particular way?

- What message is my tone of voice and body language sending to my students?

Notice that these self-evaluation questions can be about general classroom behaviors or specific responses to individual students. Teachers in the relationship-driven classroom evaluate the effectiveness and helpfulness of their behavior and beliefs in both their personal and professional lives and alter their behavior accordingly.

Administrators can assist teachers and teachers can assist students in this process. Self-evaluation is critical because it increases responsibility for change, self-control, ownership for change (changing for yourself rather than for someone else), self-awareness, and pride. Contrast self-evaluation with more traditional evaluation from an outside source. Traditional external evaluation—when you are simply told what you are doing incorrectly—can lead to defensiveness, hurt feelings, and reduced ownership. When you decide that your own behavior is not effective and make a positive change, pride is enhanced. Videotaping your classroom lessons can be a useful tool in self-evaluation. The practice of self-evaluation is consistent with the premise in psychology that we cannot change other people, only ourselves.

Student Self-Evaluation

Teachers are in a key position to assist students in the self-evaluation process. When we encourage students to judge the effectiveness of their behavior and thoughts, we increase their ownership of change, self-awareness, self-control, responsibility, sense of pride, and effective decision making. This process is contrary to what happens in many classrooms. Common practice is to tell students what is wrong with their behavior and tell them to change. Most adults and students get defensive when we take this direct approach. While a direct approach is sometimes necessary with certain difficult students, with most students it means a missed opportunity to increase self-control and responsibility. A most critical distinction in the relationship-driven approach is between self-control and external control. We should strive to teach our students self-control because it is the basis for responsibility. External control is the basis for obedience. With external control, students are dependent on the presence of an adult to behave appropriately. However, responsible students make effective choices with or without an adult present.

A detailed description of the process of student self-evaluation is in Chapter 7. For now, here are a few examples of questions teachers can ask students to encourage them to self-evaluate their own behavior:

- Is your behavior helping or hurting you? Is it getting you what you want?

- Is that behavior helping or hurting the class?

- Is not turning in your homework helping your grade?

These questions and the answers may seem obvious to us. However, students may have never examined the effectiveness of their behavior. These questions can lead to a discussion of a plan for more effective choices.

When teachers ask these questions in a calm and friendly tone, the teacher-student relationship is preserved. When tempted to give an order or solve a problem for a student, it is often helpful to ask a question instead. The relationship-driven approach encourages asking questions because it facilitates responsibility, self-control, self-awareness, and decision making while reducing the defensiveness of the student and preserving the relationship. Self-evaluation is not only for behaviors but also for beliefs that have a strong influence on our behaviors. The next section turns to the related topic of examining or self-evaluating our beliefs.

EXAMINING BELIEFS

An effective teacher understands how perceptions or beliefs influence behavior. For example, if we hold the belief that all students should be treated equally, this may hinder our flexibility in dealing with a student who is not experiencing success or has diverse learning needs. If, on the other hand, we hold the belief that all students should be treated as individuals, we are likely to be more amenable to adapting instruction.

We all have certain deeply held beliefs about our profession and how to educate children. These beliefs not only influence our behavior but also may hinder our consideration of new strategies and ideas. If our goal is to prioritize teacher-student relationships and other strategies that enhance resiliency, we must carefully examine our own belief systems. Ideally, this is an ongoing process, not just a one-time exam. I recommend that you reflect on what you believe and ask yourself a deceivingly simple question, "Does it help to look at things in this way?" This question can also be useful for students who might hold beliefs that are influencing their behavior. What follows are some beliefs and common discipline myths and assumptions that are related to relationship-driven classroom management. The beliefs are followed by some questions that might help to reshape your beliefs. I encourage you to reflect on your beliefs, what effect they have on your own behavior, and whether or not the beliefs are helpful or hurtful.

- *The goal of classroom management is to control students.* Should this be our focus or should it be to help our students develop self-control?

- *All students should be treated equally.* Is it really fair to treat all students the same? In what ways would you want your child treated differently at school? What message does this send to our students about tolerance and diversity issues? How does this statement differ from "All students should be treated as individuals"?

- *Students need to be punished to learn how to behave.* What do students actually learn when they are punished? Would you punish students to help them learn academic skills?

- *The teacher's role is not to teach what students should learn at home.* If students do not learn these critical skills at home, where might they learn them? If these skills are related to being an effective learner, should we have some responsibility in developing them?

- *Students should do as I say because I am the adult and they are children.* How does this belief influence your behavior when students do not do as you say? Does having this belief place distance between you and your students or erode mutual respect?

- *There is not enough time in the school day to worry about building relationships, resiliency, and social-emotional skills.* How might these things complement your curricular goals? Would students engage themselves more fully in learning if they believed that they mattered to the teacher and could relate well to others, influence decisions that directly impact them, succeed with adequate effort, make good choices, and overcome adversity?

COMMON MYTHS AND DANGEROUS ASSUMPTIONS

In addition to the inhibiting beliefs, some myths and assumptions that teachers and most adults hold are dangerous to children and interfere with a relationship-driven approach to classroom management. These are the myths of independence, laziness, self-esteem, and punishment.

The Independence Myth

This myth manifests in response to attempts to gain more assistance or support for a student. The independence myth is guided by the assumption that if we provide support for a student in a certain skill, they will not learn to do it independently. This assumption comes out in statements such as "If I have to constantly check his assignment book, than he will never learn to be independent." There are at least two negative ramifications with this assumption: First, becoming independent requires many different subskills. Some students may not know how or forget to write the assignments down. If these students received assistance in one or more of these subskills, they might become more independent. When students are learning academic skills, we give them more support at first and gradually phase out our support as the student gains independence with the skill. This same process is also important for behavior.

Second, do we want independent or interdependent learners in the future? It seems that business and industry are calling for learners who can access information well and can work well with others under the philosophy that many heads are better than one. Maybe we have placed too much emphasis on independence for our students, and instead more emphasis should be placed on helping them to be collaborators and not soloists (Kagan, 1994). Certainly we must be careful not to do too much for our students, which sends the following message: "You are unable to do this without someone's help." Students can and will take advantage of this and become overly dependent.

So what message do we want to send to students? By overemphasizing independence, we may be sending a mixed message. On one hand, we tell students to let us know if they need help or have any questions; on the other hand, we tell them that they need to be independent. I suggest a balance between these two extremes: we want to send the message to students that we are here to help them become more independent learners.

The Laziness Myth

Perhaps the most and hurtful and least talked about of all the myths has to do with laziness. When students will not complete work or engage in a behavior that an adult wants them to do, they are frequently labeled lazy. There are at least three negative ramifications of this assumption: First, we are often too quick to make this diagnosis—in a sense, we are being lazy when we oversimplify and fail to explore some possible reasons for the so-called lazy behaviors of our students. There are many possible explanations for why a student may be failing to produce or avoiding work. Similar to the independence myth, students may appear lazy but lack skills or subskills in the task they are being asked to complete. For example, it is not uncommon for students to do work and then fail to turn it in. Do they not turn it in because they are lazy?

Second, by stating, "This kid is just lazy," the adult shifts the responsibility from the environmental conditions that influence behavior and motivation—including the teacher behaviors—to the student. By focusing on student laziness, we may fail to examine what we are asking our students to do. Is the curriculum or task relevant, meaningful, and adequately but not too challenging for the student? Have we created an environment where the student feels safe to take risks?

Last, calling someone lazy labels the child more so than the behavior. When we attach a negative label to a student, our expectations are lowered. When we set low expectations for our students either verbally or silently, they usually live up to the low expectations. It may be more effective to view students who are nonproductive as possibly lacking in some subskill or as trying to protect themselves from looking dumb. Gifted students may avoid work not because they are afraid of looking dumb but because they are afraid of performing less than brilliant. In some cases of "laziness," there is evidence of long-standing problems and patterns of academic weaknesses. So has the child just always been "lazy," or is it possible that something is interfering with the child's performance? In almost every case, students in early elementary school are not lazy. We may get more effort from our students if we focus on encouraging and inspiring students rather than labeling them.

Many students who appear lazy struggle to understand the connection between effort and success. Rather than labeling students, a better strategy is to focus on helping students make a mental connection between their effort and the positive results. For example, when returning a paper, we could say, "Your effort is paying off" or "It seems as if you put some time and effort into this." Effective teachers help students make the connection between effort and success. Simply talking to the students about times in the past when the teacher and the student succeeded because of effort can help them make the connection.

The Self-Esteem Myth

The self-esteem myth comes from two misguided assumptions: that adults can impart self-esteem to children by what they say and do and that children must feel good about themselves. Regarding the first assumption, adults may be more powerful in diminishing self-esteem than they are in enhancing it. For example, humiliating, degrading, criticizing, and berating obviously does not build a child's self-esteem, and simply telling a child that her or she is "great," "special," or "talented" will not in itself elevate self-esteem either. This is where the second assumption comes into play. Self-esteem is neither a feeling nor is it based on feelings. Self-esteem only develops out of true competence: In simple terms, children must know that they are competent in or good at skills to have self-esteem.

Teachers can enhance self-esteem not by what they say to students as much as by helping them in recognizing and building their strengths and interests, noticing improvements, and, most of all, helping them set and reach high but attainable goals. When students do their best work or accomplish something that is challenging, they develop pride and competence. Nothing increases the self-esteem of a child as much as the pride that comes from accomplishing a personal goal. This is especially powerful when the task is one that is personally meaningful to the student or is one that the student previously thought was unattainable.

Overcoming adversity or accomplishing something in the face of frustration fosters self-esteem. Adults who try to protect children from experiencing reasonable adversity actually harm the development of self-esteem. In addition, comparisons of one child to another can erode self-esteem or erase the benefits of personal accomplishments. Comparisons are only helpful when they compare a child's present accomplishments with his or her past accomplishments. Also, self-esteem is diminished when we tell children they are good at something when they are not. This false or insincere praise hurts self-esteem.

So what does the self-esteem myth have to do with discipline? It has a great deal to do with discipline and even more to do with resilience. The danger arises when adults are fearful to correct a child because the child may feel bad and have lowered self-esteem. In addition to helping children develop areas of competence, we can assist children's self-esteem by using appropriate and consistent discipline. Withholding appropriate discipline under the guise that it will hurt self-esteem is misguided and dangerous. In fact, the opposite is true. Effective discipline leads to more inner control, which in turn can lead to success for the student. Resilient students usually have someone in their life who sets limits on their behavior. The casual reader may think this book is advocating for positive teacher-student relationships at the expense of discipline, that the two ideas are competing forces. Actually the opposite is true, both effective discipline and positive teacher-student relationships are needed for students to develop confidence and competence.

The Punishment Myth

The punishment myth is probably the most pervasive of all the myths. Punishment is defined as suppressing behavior by presenting something unpleasant or causing hurt, pain, or loss. This myth comes from the assumption that punishment deters or prevents poor behavior and that for someone to learn what not to do they must experience pain, hurt, or loss.

Our culture relies heavily on punishment to deal with a variety of social issues from crime to education. Politicians deal with crime by adding tougher sentences and penalties. Educators, when faced with an increase in targeted violence in schools, quickly moved to zero-tolerance and other punitive models. A central part of the education reform legislation No Child Left Behind is that schools will be penalized for not making steady and regular improvements. In seems like punishment is part of every solution for every problem. Our society may be blinded by this perplexing lure of punishment.

Unfortunately, punishment has many drawbacks that are often overlooked. Punishment fails to teach or model more adaptive or effective behavior. It is reactive, it suppresses but does not eliminate the behavior. It can lead to a desire for retaliation, it can lessen responsibility because the receiver of punishment focuses on the punishment and the punisher rather than the misbehavior, and it always hurts the relationship between the punisher and the one being punished. The strongest argument for reducing or eliminating punishment models is that almost every behavior that has been suppressed by punishment has also been effectively reduced by nonpunitive or positive interventions (LaVigna & Donellan, 1986). When prevention techniques—such as the ones advocated in the next chapters—are used, the need for punitive reactive measures is reduced. In addition to examining their beliefs, effective teachers use strategies that help them to maintain their enthusiasm.

STRATEGIES THAT HELP MAINTAIN TEACHER ENTHUSIASM

Effective classroom teachers communicate high expectations for their students' academic performance. In addition, effective classroom managers hold high expectations for student behavior. Expectations, like beliefs, influence our attitudes and behaviors. Expectations lead to self-fulfilling prophecies. A self-fulfilling prophecy, or Pygmalion effect, occurs when our expectations influence the outcomes of events in our lives.

Research shows that expectations affect how teachers interact with students. For example, studies found that teachers interact differently with high and low achievers (Brophy & Good, 2000). Teachers in these studies called on low achievers less and gave them less wait time to respond to questions. In addition, teachers criticized low achievers more often and gave them less praise for success, fewer positive and friendly interactions, and less attention. These studies reveal that we may be inadvertently sending a discouraging message to our students. Teacher enthusiasm is necessary to fight the tendency to set low expectations for our students. We cannot expect our students to be enthusiastic learners if we are not enthusiastic teachers.

We need to monitor our expectations for our students and practice strategies to remain enthusiastic, including stress reduction, self-motivation planning, vision planning, and optimism. Many of these strategies are easily adapted for use with students, and students can certainly benefit from strategies to effectively cope with stress.

Stress Reduction

Teaching is a very stressful job. Teachers make more important decisions, answer more questions, do more simultaneous tasking, and have more paperwork than almost any other type of professional. In addition, the pressure involved with high-stakes testing and accountability leads to additional stress. In some schools teachers may have little say in many classroom practices, which exacerbates stress. Stress reduction techniques help teachers manage stress effectively. When we practice effective stress management and are able to remain reasonably calm, we model important skills for our students. Teachers can manage their stress by using the following techniques:

- *Teach something you are passionate about each day.* Building your interests and passions into each teaching day helps to keep you enthusiastic. For example, a teacher who is passionate about character education can incorporate character quotes into her daily oral language sentences.

- *Consult with positive colleagues.* It is hard enough to stay positive and enthusiastic without the influence of negative peers, so avoid colleagues who are pessimistic, negatively label students, and set low expectations for students. The teachers' planning room needs to be a positive reprieve from the rigors of teaching, not a breeding ground for negativity. Consult with peers to determine what is working with challenging students instead of what is not working.

- *Exercise.* Exercise is basic to wellness and almost all relaxation plans. Moderate exercise is positively related to numerous physical and mental health factors and can even help prevent and treat depression and anxiety.

- *Progressive muscle relaxation.* Progressive muscle relaxation is a great tool for reducing stress and anxiety in both children and adults. Progressive muscle relaxation is a fancy name for systematically tensing and relaxing the muscles in your body. Typically, you start at one end of your body and work up or down, tensing your muscles for 5 to 10 seconds and then relaxing the same muscle for 5 to 10 seconds. Progressive muscle relaxation is often paired with other relaxation strategies, such as deep breathing and positive mental imagery, to increase the relaxation response. While practicing progressive muscle relaxation, it is important that you focus on the present task (tensing and relaxing) instead of letting your mind drift toward the past and the future.

Self-Motivation Planning

Self-motivation plans are another way we model important skills to our students. If we would like to motivate our students, it may be useful to improve our own motivation and energy. The following are 10 suggestions for developing a self-motivation plan, adapted from Wubbolding (1996):

Choose every day to deepen a relationship with one person. This implies a conscious decision to smile, to take an interest in someone, or to do a favor for someone.

Choose every day to learn more about another person. Inquire about what the person likes, thinks, feels, wants, and so on.

Choose every day to do something you've been procrastinating about.

Choose every day to laugh at yourself. Present your ideas as your ideas and not as absolute dogmas that everyone must believe.

Choose every day to take responsibility for your successes and failures. Take responsibility instead of blaming the boss, your students, the government, parents, or others.

Choose every day to read your own personal philosophy of life or education. Do some research and find a positive and hopeful description of what you believe is important.

Choose every day to read some positive literature. What goes into our minds influences who we are.

Choose to select something you want and begin to take small steps to achieve it.

Choose slogans, mantras, and prayers to repeat each day.

Choose every day to contribute to your financial future.

Vision Planning

A vision drives our behavior and student behavior toward a goal. When we do not have a vision for where we would like to go, we often go in too many directions or get lost. Vision planning involves thinking about long-term goals for your students and classroom. It involves thinking about what you would like your students to have learned by the end of the year or at some point in time.

These goals could be academic, social-emotional, or behavioral. Some specific examples of goals for students are that each student is able to name the branches of government and its function, develop skills for lifelong learning, learn how to resolve conflicts, learn the power of a positive attitude, and learn how to handle setbacks. Notice that these goals are related to one's personal philosophy and the age and skill of your students, and they also may be related to the curriculum.

The students should be aware of these long-term goals and may have a role in developing and posting them in the classroom. When we have a vision for our students, we have a built-in system for decision making: Is this going to lead us in the direction of our goals or take us in another direction?

Optimism

Optimism is remaining realistically hopeful that events will work out. Optimism is much more than positive thinking. Optimists explain negative events that happen to them in temporary, realistic, specific, and nonpersonal ways; pessimists, on the other hand, explain negative events in permanent, unrealistically negative, generalized, and personalized ways.

When students exhibit challenging behaviors, optimistic teachers remain positive that the student can learn more effective behaviors in the future. An exaggerated pessimistic response to a challenging behavior might be "He will never [permanent] learn. He always [generalized] misbehaves and is driving me [personal] nuts." A more optimistic response would be "Since he hasn't yet [temporary] learned appropriate behavior when we are in the hallway [specific], he will have to practice this behavior [nonpersonal]." Optimistic teachers believe that their students will start to develop more effective behaviors and resist the temptation to see weaknesses as permanent.

Optimists routinely challenge or dispute their pessimistic or irrational thoughts. They dispute these thoughts much in the same way that they would if they were disagreeing or arguing with someone else. Practicing and learning to dispute negative thoughts and pessimism have been shown to predict success at work, at home, in sports, in politics, and at school. In addition, optimists are more resilient and resist depression more than pessimists (Seligman, 1995). Strategies to dispute beliefs are discussed in detail in Chapter 9, and teachers will find that they are able to apply these ideas to both their students and their own personal growth. When we manage our stress effectively, use self-motivation planning and vision planning, and maintain optimism, we are able to maintain enthusiasm, a positive attitude, and high expectations for our students.

SUMMARY OF MAIN POINTS

- Relationship-driven teachers continually strive to model the social skills that they would like their students to develop.

- Relationship-driven teachers practice self-evaluation by taking an honest look at the effectiveness and helpfulness of their wants, behaviors, and beliefs, both in the classroom and in their personal lives.

- Relationship-driven teachers carefully examine how the myths of independence, laziness, self-esteem, and punishment can hurt their students.

- To maintain positive teacher enthusiasm and high student expectations it is beneficial to practice stress reduction techniques, self-motivation planning, vision planning, and optimistic thinking.

QUESTIONS FOR
DISCUSSION AND SELF-EVALUATION

1. Think back on a favorite teacher that you may have had. What personal attributes did this teacher have that you would like to emulate?

2. What are some other common beliefs that influence teacher behavior and impact students?

3. What is one advantage that self-evaluation has over traditional external evaluation?

4. How does self-evaluation increase self-control?

5. Does the personal habits of teachers make any difference in their effectiveness in the classroom?

ACTION PLAN

As a result of something that I learned in this chapter I plan to (be specific in your answer):

_____

_____

_____

RECOMMENDED RESOURCES

Brophy, J., & Good, T. (2000). *Looking in classrooms* (8th ed.). Boston: Allyn & Bacon. This book is often used as a college text and is an excellent source for practical and research-proven classroom techniques for learning and behavior.

Davis, M., Eshelman, E., & McKay, M. (2000). *The relaxation and stress reduction workbook* (5th ed.). Oakland, CA: New Harbinger. This book provides step-by-step instructions for stress reduction, including deep breathing, progressive muscle relaxation, visual imagery, meditation, and thought-stopping techniques.

Glasser, W. (1998). *Choice theory: A new psychology of personal freedom.* New York: HarperCollins. This book assists teachers in self-evaluation and self-improvement and also provides insights into understanding and educating students.

Wubbolding, R., & Brickell, J. (2001). *A set of directions for putting and keeping your life together.* Minneapolis, MN: Educational Media Corporation. This book applies the ideas of reality therapy to self-improvement and helps teachers deal with excuses and make effective plans to satisfy their basic needs. This book takes complex psychological concepts and translates them into a simple and straightforward language.

CHAPTER THREE

Proactive Classroom Management Strategies

"Every minute spent in proactive classroom management, time actually spent teaching rules and procedures at the beginning of the year, pays off every day for the rest of the year."

—Evertson and Harris (2003, p. 205)

CHAPTER OBJECTIVES

In this chapter the reader will learn:

- Strategies for preventing misbehavior and improving learning
- Strategies for teaching procedures, routines, and expectations
- Strategies for devising and teaching classroom rules
- Strategies for designing and maintaining a positive classroom climate
- Strategies for designing a need-satisfying classroom

STRATEGIES FOR PREVENTING MISBEHAVIOR

A prevention-oriented approach to classroom management is more effective than a corrective or reactive approach. Effective classroom managers prevent misbehavior, so they do not have to rely solely on reactive measures. Reactive measures without adequate prevention can significantly increase the amount of time a teacher spends on discipline issues (Brophy & Good, 2000). It is wise for teachers to put much effort in setting up a prevention-oriented classroom at the beginning of the school year because this ultimately saves time for the teacher in the long run (Evertson & Harris, 2003).

Why Do Students Misbehave?

Students misbehave for a myriad of reasons. Student behavior is not completely random and usually serves a function or purpose for the individual (Kottler, 2002). It is important, as a relationship-driven teacher, to understand these reasons, so you can prevent the conditions that cause misbehavior from occurring in the classroom. While this is not an exhaustive list, students may misbehave under the following conditions:

1. The student has unmet basic physical and psychological needs.

2. The student does not know what the teacher's expectations are.

3. The student does not know how or when to display the appropriate behavior.

4. The student is unaware of his or her own behavior.

5. The student receives some pleasant outcome from the misbehavior.

6. The student avoids some unpleasant outcome from the misbehavior.

7. The teacher-student relationship is strained or negative.

The relationship-driven classroom management approach strives to eliminate these conditions by planning and teaching procedures, routines, and expectations; by devising and teaching effective classroom rules; by creating a positive classroom climate; and by designing a need-satisfying classroom. In upcoming chapters I discuss additional strategies to prevent misbehavior, such as enhancing relationships, social-emotional skills, and academic success.

STRATEGIES FOR TEACHING PROCEDURES, ROUTINES, AND EXPECTATIONS

Procedures are steps or behaviors that allow the class to accomplish tasks in a smooth and efficient manner. Research has found that effective classroom managers plan, establish, and teach procedures for such things as bringing materials to class, turning in homework, completing makeup work, transitioning between activities, beginning and ending routines, participating in small-group or cooperative activities, participating in teacher-led instruction, working independently, and taking tests (Evertson & Harris, 2003). The typical classroom has a great number of procedures that students need to master. Consider how most teachers teach the procedures for a fire or emergency drill. They typically go over the procedure in detail and usually allow the students to practice the procedure. It may be helpful to teach other classroom procedures in a similar fashion.

When we reflect on classroom tasks and procedures we realize that they require that the students demonstrate a great number of subskills. For example, simply lining up to leave the classroom involves listening for a cue, clearing desks, standing up, pushing chairs in quietly, walking calmly, maintaining personal space, and lining up in a designated area.

Prior to beginning an activity or transition, effective managers explicitly teach their expectations for behavior. Once the activity begins, they monitor for compliance, give specific feedback during and after the activity, and reteach as necessary. They may teach these procedures by explaining, rehearsing, monitoring, providing feedback, and reteaching. Notice that the sequence is very much similar to the effective teaching of academic skills.

When students know prior to an activity or transition the exact expectations for behavior, misbehavior is often prevented, and learning is enhanced (Sprick, Garrison, & Howard, 1998).

Small-Group Instruction and Independent Work

What procedure should the teacher follow if he or she is planning to work with a small group of students while the rest of the other students work independently? One way to manage this issue is to tell the students to work independently and then proceed to the small group—a strategy likely to result in misbehavior. A more effective strategy would be to state and demonstrate to the students what expectations the teacher has for the students engaged in independent work. Explain to them what the objective of the activity is, what to do if they have questions, if they may talk or not, what the appropriate voice volume is, what to do if they get finished early, and what appropriate behavior would look like in this situation. Teachers prevent misbehavior by not leaving their behavioral expectations up to chance and by making them clearly understood and not assumed.

Periodically as you are working with the small group you should monitor the students engaged in independent work and provide positive recognition for compliance and reteaching or corrective procedures for noncompliance. When students do not meet teacher procedural expectations, teachers teach or reteach their expectation and ask the students to practice, much like they would teach if a student made an academic error.

Sprick and colleagues (1998) provide an excellent methodology for teaching expectations to students in their CHAMPs program. The CHAMPs acronym is used as a tool to make sure the expectations are explicit prior to beginning each task or transition. The *C* stands for Conversation (Are students permitted to talk?), the *H* stands for Help (What should students do if they need assistance?), the *A* stands for Activity (What is the objective and end product?), and the *P* stands for Participation (How do students show that they are fully participating?).

Classroom Transitions

Ineffective transitions can lead to lost instructional time and misbehavior. This usually occurs because transitions are often unstructured. A prerequisite to effective transitions is that the teacher be prepared for the next activity and have materials readily accessible. Teachers can enhance the structure of transitions by teaching clear behavioral expectations, consistently practicing and following transition routines, and regularly acknowledging successful transitions. For example, when papers need to be collected, the teacher could explain that papers will be passed forward to the front of the row, designate a person to collect the papers from each row to deliver to the teacher, state whether talking is permitted, and state the appropriate volume of students' voices. Students are then given appropriate feedback. Another simple example is to make sure you tell students what to do when they finish their work. Many potential problems can be avoided using this strategy.

Although the process of teaching expectations for every transition may seem tedious, it will ultimately save time since much time is wasted repeating directions and dealing with slow and chaotic transitions and misbehavior. Generally speaking, this process is used more at the beginning of the year, after long breaks, and with younger students. However, assuming that older students know the procedures is not as wise as checking their understanding and practicing if necessary.

The relationship-driven classroom manager frequently asks, "Do I teach expectations for procedures and transitions directly and have my students demonstrated mastery?" Devising and teaching effective classroom rules is also important in preventing misbehavior, and I discuss that aspect of relationship-driven management in the following section.

CLASSROOM RULES

Effective classroom rules are necessary to a smooth-running classroom. Students need to know what behavior is acceptable and unacceptable and the consequences likely to follow unacceptable behavior. Some discipline approaches advocate having specific consequences for each rule. This really is not necessary and can cause difficulty later when you want to individualize for a particular student. Instead, it may be helpful to discuss with students some examples of consequences that might be used.

Figure 3.1 Classroom Rules and Expectations

LIFE RULES	CLASSROOM EXPECTATIONS
Be prompt	Meet deadlines.
Be prepared	Have materials. Listen for
Participate	instructions. Follow
	instructions.
	Be a part of discussion. Complete
Show respect	work. Stay engaged.
	Honor self and others. Value
Be responsible	property.
	Accept ownership. Plan more
	effective behavior.

SOURCE: Reprinted with permission from Bodine and Crawford (1999).

Number and Content of Classroom Rules

Classroom rules should be few in number (between three and six), expressed in positive as opposed to negative terms (e.g., "Students will be on time" vs. "No tardiness"), sensible, observable, and consistent with school rules. Be careful not to confuse classroom rules with procedures: There are many classroom procedures but only a few classroom rules; however, classroom rules often involve procedures. Classroom rules should be posted in the room in bold and large print. In addition, it is advisable to send a copy of the classroom rules home for parents to review with their children.

Classroom rules usually address bringing necessary materials to class, treating other people and their property appropriately, participating, following schoolwide rules, and talking at appropriate times and appropriate volume. Figures 3.1 and 3.2 give two examples of classroom rules. Notice how the example of classroom rules in Figure 3.2 uses questions. This strategy is consistent with self-evaluation and developing self-control. Teachers should discuss and brainstorm with students these concepts to make them more specific and concrete. Once students understand the concepts and why they are important, the teacher is able to ask the appropriate question to the student to fit the misbehavior. For example, if a student pokes another student, the teacher could ask the misbehaving student, "Is that being kind or considerate?"

Figure 3.2   Getting Along in the Classroom

Cooperation—We listen, share, and do our part.

Consideration—We help others out when we can, say only good things about and to others, and treat people with respect.

Conservation—Property and environment are important. We take care of things and do not destroy them.

Safety—We learn best in a school where no one gets hurt. Safety means we are careful not to hurt others, and we solve our problems by talking them through.

- Cooperation—Is it helpful?
- Consideration—Is it kind?
- Conservation—Could it waste or destroy anything?
- Safety—Could anyone get hurt?

SOURCE: Adapted from Ludwig and Mentley (1997).

The most important aspect of devising classroom rules is that they are taught to the students, much like an academic skill, at the beginning of the year and periodically reviewed thereafter. Once again it is important not to assume that students understand and can follow the rules right from the start. If the classroom rule is to use appropriate voices at appropriate times, the students may need to practice appropriate volume in different situations. For example, they may need to practice using both 6- and 12-inch voices in appropriate situations. We must realize that although this takes valuable time, especially at the beginning of the year, it will pay dividends in the long run.

Discussions about the value of rules in society, sports, the workplace, and so on help students understand that these behaviors will help them meet their needs and increase their likelihood of success. Some teachers involve their students in the creation of the classroom rules, a practice that builds student ownership, develops a spirit of cooperation, and satisfies students' need for choice in what happens to them. In addition, allowing students to participate in rule development facilitates student understanding and puts students and teachers on the same side.

Rights and Responsibilities

A strategy that builds self-control and responsibility is using the concept of rights and responsibilities in your classroom rule development. A right is a freedom, and a responsibility is an expectation for one's behavior. For example, students have the right to be safe and the responsibility to make the classroom safe by not behaving in an aggressive, dangerous, or bullying manner. These abstract concepts may need to be made more explicit for younger students. For example, students have the right to be safe and to not be hit, kicked, or threatened; they have the responsibility to not hit, kick, or threaten other students.

It is important for students to help create these rights and responsibilities. After their creation, teachers must teach students the importance of exercising their rights without interfering with the rights of others, a concept that builds skills for conflict resolution and principles of democracy. The drawbacks to creating rights and responsibilities in partnership with students are that the process is time consuming and the class is operating without a set of rules during the development stage. However, autocratic approaches, though effective in the short run, are coercive, put students and teachers on opposite sides, and lead more to obedience than to responsible and cooperative behavior. Bodine and Crawford (1999) is an excellent resource for more information on using classroom rights and responsibilities.

POSITIVE CLASSROOM CLIMATE

Classroom climate is difficult to define but ultimately has to do with emotions and relationships in the classroom. A positive classroom climate is critical to any discipline or management program in increasing academic learning and preventing behavior problems before they disrupt the learning environment (Wang, Haertel, & Walberg, 1994). How a student perceives the classroom climate can have a strong influence on achievement and prosocial behavior (Solomon, Battistich, Kim, & Watson, 1997). In a review of the literature, Battistich, Solomon, Watson, and Schaps (1997) found that a student's sense of membership in a caring and supportive learning community enhanced prosocial behavior, connection and commitment to school, motivation to engage in learning, and valuing of learning. The relationship-driven teacher builds and maintains a positive classroom climate by praising students and using strategies that increase emotional safety and put the teacher and the students on the same side. Striving for positive relationships in the classroom, the subject of Chapter 4, is also a key ingredient in a positive classroom climate.

Emotional Safety

Positive classroom climates also need to be emotionally safe. Threats and fear have a negative effect on student learning; hence, students learn better when they feel emotionally and physically safe. The following conditions, adapted from Bluestein (2001), occur in classrooms when emotional safety is met:

- A sense of belonging and acceptance
- Being valued and recognized for one's unique talents and skills
- A clear understanding of expectations
- Predictability of consequences and freedom from arbitrary and unexpected punishment
- Freedom from harassment, labeling, name calling, teasing, and criticism
- Freedom to make choices and influence one's own learning
- Freedom from prejudice based on physical appearance, racial, sexual, cultural, athletic, academic, and social characteristics
- Freedom to be able to express one's own feelings and opinions without fear

Teachers play a critical role in creating this climate. Teachers can increase students' sense of community by emphasizing prosocial values, eliciting student expression of ideas, encouraging cooperation, and displaying warmth and supportiveness (Solomon et al., 1997). Bluestein (2001) describes the following characteristics of teachers who are able to create a caring community of learners: empathetic, responsive, authentic, accepting, and warm; ability to display genuine appreciation for students' opinions, tailor discussions to students' frame of reference, and have a strong belief in the students' potential.

A relationship-driven classroom is sensitive to the effects fear of mistakes can have on the emotions and risk-taking behaviors of students. How the teacher responds to academic and behavioral mistakes is very important. If the teacher focuses on the process and individual mastery more than the outcome or competition, students get the message that it is safe to take academic risks and will even ask more questions in front of their peers (Ryan, Gheen, & Midgley, 1998). Obviously, humiliation, embarrassment, or any behavior that causes a student to lose face in front of his or her peers is contrary to a positive and emotionally safe classroom climate.

I once worked with a teacher who would pass back exams in order of the grade received. Those with high grades would get their papers first, and those with the lowest grades would get theirs last. Similarly, some teachers post grades or comment to the entire class about low scores. These teachers intend for the students with low grades to want to avoid embarrassment and work harder.

Negative motivation, or the idea that students will do better to avoid embarrassment, is not only contrary to emotional safety but is also contrary to learning and brain research. Fear and threat, just like punishment, activate more primitive areas of the brain (self-protection), which in a way short-circuit or inhibit higher cortical areas critical in learning (Goleman, 1998). Negative motivational techniques increase the fear and stress that the student feels when taking tests in the future. High stress, emotion, and threats do not enhance learning but breed resentment and avoidance and hurt the teacher-student relationship.

Strategies That Put
Teacher and Student on the Same Side

Some autocratic teachers may not realize that they are creating an adversarial relationship in the classroom. When students have little say about what, how, and with whom learning will take place, they feel less ownership and connection to the class and the work. When we give students a say in certain conditions of learning, we build student ownership and involvement in the class and enhance classroom climate. The students begin to view the classroom as "ours." When we ask students their impression of the class, their learning, and how the teacher could make it better, we build ownership and cooperation. As Kagan (1994) states, "Because they are asked to reflect on what the teacher could do to help them learn more, they assume the role of coach or helper to the teacher, and become more identified with reaching the goals of learning" (p. 94).

It is not uncommon for adults and students to have differing opinions about the classroom and school climate. It is of little benefit if the adults feel a sense of community or positive classroom climate when the students do not share this perception. Survey research found differing perceptions of school and classroom climate when rated by the teacher and also by the student. In fact, in a survey of 100,000 students in the United States, 76% did not perceive their school as having a caring and supportive school climate (Benson, Galbraith, & Espeland, 1998). When we request feedback from our students, we send a caring message and put the teacher and the student on the same side. The Relationship-Driven Classroom Assessment Scale–Student Form, discussed in Chapter 10, is a tool for teachers to assess the perceptions of their students.

In addition to obtaining student feedback, allowing students to make decisions about the classroom puts teachers and students on the same side. For example, students can make decisions about their own personalized learning goals, based on more general topic objectives, and can help decide on class rewards, classroom rules, room arrangement, bulletin boards, class meetings, projects, instructional formats, and schedules. Allowing students a say in class decision making helps satisfy their need for power and freedom and also increases their motivation to learn.

A spirit of cooperation in the classroom puts teachers and students on the same side. Ideally, a balance should be used between competition and cooperation in the classroom. In competition, there are winners and losers, and some students become anxious in competitive situations and choose to withdraw. However, in cooperative classroom contexts, all students are winners—that is, "we" is better than "I." Cooperative learning can be beneficial, especially if the teacher has spent sufficient time teaching the students acceptable behavior for group work and stresses both individual and group accountability (Kagan, 1994). Cooperative learning groups can reduce some of the negative effects of competition, and students obtain the added benefit of learning social skills and collaboration. Interested readers are referred to Kagan (1994) for more information on cooperative learning.

Encouraging and Effective Praise

The relationship-driven teacher uses encouraging and effective praise to enhance the classroom climate. Praise, when used effectively and frequently, can improve classroom climate and improve behavior. Although research has documented the effectiveness of verbal praise on student behavior and achievement, teachers use it sparingly. For example, in the average classroom teachers deliver a negative verbal reprimand every 2 to 5 minutes. They deliver a positive statement about every 20 minutes (Algozzine & Ysseldyke, 1997). When we acknowledge negative behavior more than positive behavior, what message does it send to our students? Effective teachers realize that adults and students need to be positively recognized and praised to maintain their behavior and motivation. Similarly, both adults and students are discouraged when they are only noticed for their failures or mistakes.

Effective and encouraging praise is genuine, specific about the accomplishment, attributes accomplishments more to effort than to ability, and compares the present accomplishment to accomplishments in the individual's past. Ineffective praise is often vague (e.g., "good job"), focused on ability only, and compares the individual's accomplishment with others' accomplishments (Brophy & Good, 2000). Although difficult in practice, we should avoid praising students by using repetitive, bland, or insincere phrases. Praise should not be given for completing simple tasks or for simply completing an activity, regardless of the result. Poor examples of praise include "Good job," "You're so smart," "I am so proud of you," and "What a beautiful painting." More effective praise includes the following: "Your hard work is really paying off in your scores on your division papers. You went from getting four problems correct on the last quiz to getting eight correct on this one," and "The colors you used in your painting are great." When praising students it is helpful to note the effort or process that the students used instead of only focusing on the final result or grade; however, ideally, both the effort and result are mentioned in the praise statement.

Another example involves younger students, who frequently ask if they did a good job on their artwork. An example of ineffective praise in this situation would be "Yes, you are a great painter." An encouraging response might be "You seem to really enjoy painting," "You really worked hard on your painting," "Tell me what you think of your painting," or "I can see you put a lot of work into this." Another excellent strategy is to ask students how they would like to be praised for their accomplishments. For example, some students dislike being praised in front of their peers; others prefer a more private form of praise.

Praise, if used incorrectly, can reduce intrinsic motivation (i.e., the desire to accomplish a task because of the task itself) and lead to an external locus of control—a student who is dependent on praise from an adult or getting something for performing the task. These children are only motivated to engage in tasks if it will get a reaction out of an adult. In other words, they behave to get something in return.

The child who is overly praised for ability more so than effort may have considerable difficulty in the future when criticized. If they are praise dependent, they may give up easily or limit their endeavors to those tasks that provide a guarantee of praise. These children find ways to protect themselves from criticism and mistakes. This concept is also revealed in the case of some gifted children, who at very early ages receive extreme praise by adults with phrases such as "You are so smart," "You are brilliant," and "You are an excellent reader." While all these statements may be true, they too may set up this child for disappointment and defensiveness in the future and may manifest in the child avoiding tasks that may be very challenging for fear of failure or less than brilliance. Instead of viewing grades in school as measures of current performance, gifted students view grades as measures of their ability, and, as a result, some gifted children take exhaustive self-protective and avoidance measures that can lead to school underachievement or even failure.

NEED SATISFACTION

Relationship-driven classrooms strive to meet the basic psychological needs of the student. Glasser (1998) asserts that there are five basic psychological needs of all individuals: belonging, power, freedom, fun, and survival. He describes these basic needs as they relate to his theory of human behavior, once called control theory but now called choice theory. Choice theory helps us to understand how our behavior and the behavior of our students are related to the satisfaction of the five basic needs. All behavior is chosen to fulfill one or more of these basic needs, and we are responsible for our own choices. In addition, we are motivated from within to satisfy our needs. This is very different from what Glasser calls external control psychology, which states that we are motivated by events outside of us, such as stimuli, other people, rewards, and punishments.

The distinction between choice theory and external control psychology is critical in classroom management that is designed to prevent misbehavior and enhance relationships. Choice theory asserts that we are unable to control another person's behavior, only our own. If we coerce or try to make others change or do something they do not want to do, we can increase resistance to change and hurt our relationship with the individual. Take a minute to think about how you feel when other people try to get you to do something that you do not want to do.

Basic Needs

Understanding the basic needs and how they influence behavior is critical in preventing behavior problems in the classroom. What follows is a brief description of each of the basic needs and how they are satisfied and compromised:

• *Belonging.* The belonging need is satisfied when one has love, involvement, and meaningful relationships with significant others. This need is compromised when individuals are lonely and do not feel accepted or loved.

• *Power.* The power need, which involves competence, self-control, and achievement, is satisfied when a person achieves something or gains recognition for success. This need is compromised when a person experiences little success or positive recognition from others.

• *Freedom.* The need for freedom is satisfied when people are able to make choices and have influence over what happens to them. This need can be compromised when individuals have no or little say in what, when, how, and with whom tasks are to be done. This need is closely related to the resiliency protective factor of having opportunities to participate and contribute.

- *Fun.* This need involves laughing, creating, playing, and learning, and it is compromised when an individual has diminished opportunities for laughing, creating, playing, and learning.

- *Survival.* This need is satisfied through feeling secure that physical needs such as food, shelter, and safety will be met. This need is compromised when one feels physically and psychologically unsafe.

Compromised Basic Needs

We are all born with the same basic psychological needs, and we all have different wants based on these basic needs. These wants make up images or pictures in our brain, which is called our quality world. Different people choose different ways to meet these needs. At some level we are always comparing what we want and what we are getting. If there is balance between what we want and what we are getting, we feel in control and satisfied. If there is little balance between what we want and what we are getting, we feel pain, frustration, and lack of control. This frustration causes us to act or behave in such a way to reduce the frustration and pain.

People can choose or attempt effective and ineffective behaviors to get their needs met and reduce the frustration or imbalance. This behavior is our best attempt at satisfying our needs at a given moment in time. This is one of the most important concepts for us as educators to understand: If we perceive the ineffective behaviors of our students as their best attempt at meeting their own needs, and not purposeful attempts to frustrate us, we will be able to remain calm and encourage the students toward better ways to go about meeting their needs. The self-evaluation process is the cornerstone of choice theory, with the goal being for the person to take an honest look at what they want and the effectiveness of their behavior in getting them what they want.

Another important concept from choice theory is the quality world. The quality world involves specific images in the brain of what students want. The basic needs are the same for each individual, but what each person wants to satisfy that particular need fluctuates and differs from person to person. Teachers can help students to acquire quality world pictures of the class, subject, or even the teacher. When teachers establish positive relationships with students, they enter the students' quality world. Even if the particular subject matter is not in the quality world of the student, if the teacher is, motivation will be enhanced.

Examples of Compromised Basic Needs in the Classroom

Some classroom examples may help conceptualize the importance of these basic needs. The first example involves Frank. Frank is acting up in the classroom, and he continues to do so, despite many consequences and trips to the principal's office. After talking with Frank it became evident that he desires more friends and more activities with friends. We could conjecture that his inappropriate behavior is an attempt at reducing his pain and frustration due to his unmet need for belonging and fun. Frank chose ineffective ways to gain friendships and fun, although he did get some negative attention when the other students laughed at his classroom antics. Other than punishing Frank for his behavior, how might we help him to more effectively satisfy his need to belong and have fun? We could suggest social skills training, find him a mentor, or suggest an extracurricular activity. A teacher familiar with choice theory and self-evaluation would ask Frank if his behavior is helping him get what he wants and then direct him to an appropriate behavior.

Another example involves Jamie, who has not been turning in her homework. She has experienced the consequences of low grades and punishments at home. Jamie has many friends and is very social, and a review of her school records reveals that she has been experiencing low grades for the past three years. We might conjecture that Jamie has a frustrated power need (competence and achievement) and has chosen to get her needs met by focusing on socializing and avoiding schoolwork. How could we assist her in more effective ways to get her power needs satisfied? A self-evaluation question to ask Jamie would be "Is not doing your homework helping you to get what you want or hurting you?" A second question could be "How do you see me helping you get what you want?" We also could find ways to adapt her schoolwork or offer her more learning support until she meets with more success. In both of these examples, misbehavior may have been prevented if the classrooms were rich in providing for belonging and fun, in Frank's case, and power (achievement) in Jamie's case.

Teaching Students How to Satisfy Basic Needs

In classrooms where basic needs are satisfied, students are less likely to negatively act out. Students in these classrooms are fulfilling their needs without infringing on the rights of others and will work hard for those they like and care for (belonging), for those they respect and who respect them (power), for those with whom they laugh (fun), for those who allow them to think and act for themselves (freedom), and for those who help them make their own lives secure (survival) (Glasser, 1998). The more that all five of the basic needs are satisfied in the classroom, the more students will strive to do quality work and exhibit quality behavior.

Readers who are interested in more information on reality therapy and choice theory are referred to Glasser (1998), who recommends that teachers as well as students of all ages learn about the basic needs and choice theory. There are a number of good resources on teaching the basic needs to students of all ages (Glasser & Glasser, 1999). What follows are some general classroom strategies and characteristics that can assist in satisfying student basic needs. In the next chapter the focus goes to enhancing relationships in the classroom, which is key to the love and belonging need.

Love and Belonging

- Establishing a caring environment
- Establishing warm, personal, positive relationships with students
- Preventing and responding to teasing, bullying, and exclusion of students
- Teaching conflict resolution skills to maintain friendships
- Teaching social skills and using cooperative learning to build a sense of belonging

Power

- Creating opportunities and conditions for academic and behavioral success and accomplishment for all students

- Conducting individualized goal setting and evaluation
- Helping students self-evaluate their performance and behavior
- Providing frequent positive feedback and recognition
- Giving students numerous responsibilities or jobs within the classroom

Freedom

- Giving students a voice in what they learn and how they complete assignments
- Requiring students to design a plan for improvement when a problem occurs
- Taking students seriously in planning lessons, projects, classroom rules, and consequences
- Allowing students to have input in creating rules and consequences
- Giving students free time during the school day to choose from a variety of learning options

Fun

- Creating learning experiences that are fun, creative, relevant, and meaningful
- Welcoming physical activity
- Allowing and expecting talking and laughter
- Giving students a wide variety of choices in extracurricular activities
- Including students' interests in curricular planning

SUMMARY OF MAIN POINTS

- Teachers can prevent misbehavior by establishing and teaching classroom procedures, transitions, and rules prior to activities. They teach these procedures in much the same manner as they would teach academic skills.

- Teachers can create a positive classroom climate by ensuring emotional safety, by using strategies that put the teacher and student on the same side, and by using encouraging praise.

• Effective praise is recognizing the students' accomplishments in a specific way that focuses on the effort and improvement involved.

• Choice theory offers the classroom teacher a framework for understanding behavior and motivation. When the classroom is designed to satisfy the basic needs of belonging, power, freedom, fun, and survival, students are positively motivated and less likely to misbehave. When students do misbehave it is seen as the students' best attempt to meet their needs, not a personal affront to the teacher.

QUESTIONS FOR DISCUSSION AND SELF-EVALUATION

1. Is it really necessary to teach procedures and expectations for each activity and transition?

2. Do students feel safe from threat emotionally and physically in your classroom or school?

3. How is thinking and learning impaired when one is feeling stressed, threatened, or fearful?

4. Why is it important and what are some effective ways to obtain feedback from your students about their perceptions of the classroom?

5. How might designing your classroom to satisfy the basic needs prevent student misbehavior?

ACTION PLAN

As a result of something that I learned in this chapter I plan to (be specific in your answer):

_____

_____

_____

RECOMMENDED RESOURCES

Bluestein, J. (2001). *Creating emotionally safe schools: A guide for educators and parents.* Deerfield Beach, FL: Health Communications. This book provides insight into how emotional safety is connected to learning and how it is often overlooked due to an emphasis on physical safety.

Glasser, W. (1998). *Choice theory: A new psychology of personal Freedom.* New York: HarperCollins. This book provides the reader with a thorough understanding of choice theory and its applications to life, work, school, and community.

Ludwig, S., & Mentley, K. (1997). *Quality is the key: Stories from Huntington Woods School.* Wyoming, MI: KWM Educational Services. This book describes how one school implemented the ideas of choice theory to become the first designated Glasser Quality School.

Sprick, R., Garrison, M., & Howard, L. (1998). *CHAMPs: A proactive and positive approach to classroom management.* Longmont, CO: Sopris West. This book provides extensive and detailed ideas for planning and teaching classroom behavioral expectations.

CHAPTER FOUR

Strengthening Relationships With Students

"The teacher-student relationship is easily lost in a confusing web of rules, limits, and required objectives."

—Rogers and Frieberg (1994, p. 33)

CHAPTER OBJECTIVES

In this chapter the reader will learn:

- The rationale for prioritizing positive teacher-student relationships
- How relationships and interactions influence student behavior
- How to build relationships despite time constraints
- The distinction between and importance of both positive and personal teacher-student relationships
- The difference between relationship blasters and builders
- How to create a balance between being firm, fair, and friendly

THE RATIONALE FOR POSITIVE
TEACHER-STUDENT RELATIONSHIPS

Positive relationships at school and in the classroom are in many ways prerequisites for effective learning and behavior (Pianta, 1999). In addition, teacher-student relationships are influential in student exploration and academic mastery (Birch & Ladd, 1997), students' handling of peer relationships (Howes, Matheson, & Hamilton, 1994) and emotional experiences (Lynch & Cicchetti, 1992), students' self-regulation (Pianta, 1997), and student motivation (Mendler, 2000). In addition, research shows that having positive and caring relationships in school increases resilience and protects children from academic failure, mental illness, drug and alcohol abuse, and destructive behavior or violence (Resnick et al., 1997). William Glasser (1998), the founder of reality therapy, states that most long-term psychological problems are a result of problems in one or more significant relationships in a person's life. Therefore, when teachers create a positive and personal relationship with students, they may be preventing the development of psychological problems in their students. This research should lead us to ask if we are doing everything we can do to build positive relationships at school.

Numerous studies have examined what leads people to change in counseling and psychotherapy. Most controlled studies support the notion that the relationship between the therapist and client, or therapeutic alliance as it is called, has twice the influence of the theory or specific counseling techniques that are used (Hubble, Duncan, & Miller, 1999; Lambert, 1992). Corey (2000) elucidates the importance of the relationship in counseling and states that the quality of the therapeutic relationship is far more important than the techniques that are used: "If practitioners possess wide knowledge, both theoretical and practical, yet lack human qualities of compassion, caring, good faith, honesty, realness, and sensitivity, they are merely technicians" (p. 5). He goes on to state that if they lack these human qualities, they "do not make a significant difference in the lives of their clients."

You may be saying, "I'm not a therapist; I am a teacher." Though true, the two roles often have common goals. Both involve human relationships and goals of learning and change and both employ special techniques to lead the client or student to learn and change. If relationships are that influential in psychotherapy, doesn't it follow that they would also be important in learning and school? Effective teaching techniques may lose some of their impact when positive teacher-student relationships are lacking (Pianta, 1999). Therefore, when we neglect relationships, we fail to tap a substantial factor in student learning, behavior, resilience, and quality of life.

Relationships Influence Behavior

Behavior does not occur in isolation. In reality, there is always an interaction or relationship between student and teacher that must not be overlooked when thinking about behavior. In other words, both teacher and student influence each other's behavior. Behavior is multifaceted and multidetermined—that is, a person's behavior rarely has one sole cause. Understanding the complex nature of behavior and the reciprocal nature of relationships assists us in not blaming the student or the teacher for the problems that may arise.

According to Pianta (1999), although both the teacher and the student are responsible for their own behavior, the teacher is more capable of change and has more behavioral choices at their disposal than does a student. Therefore, teacher change (improving the climate, improving the relationship, altering responses to behavior or perception of the student or problem) is more efficacious than solely focusing on changing the student. This is consistent with choice theory discussed in Chapter 3. Choice theory holds as one of its major tenets that we are unable to control the behavior of others. In other words, we may get better results out of evaluating and changing our own behavior rather than putting all our efforts into changing our students' behavior.

Building Relationships With Difficult Students

Although I have witnessed numerous positive and negative examples of these interaction effects, one stands out in my mind. I worked with a middle school student who was displaying chronic underachievement and behavior difficulties. This student was in the midst of much family stress. His parents were in the midst of a bitter separation. Despite strong ability, this student was failing all of his classes. The school had numerous meetings and tried numerous strategies to address his academic and behavioral problems. The parents hired a tutor to work with the student after school, but the work that was completed in tutoring would somehow get lost before it got to the classroom teacher. None of the interventions seemed to be working.

Interestingly, we did not see much change in this student until after he went on a school-sponsored weekend ski trip. He came to my office immediately upon arrival Monday morning to tell me about his trip, and he also said, "One of [my] teachers actually likes me." He was unusually excited to tell me about his trip, and he went on to tell me about conversing with this teacher on the bus and the fun they had on the trip. I was curious about how this connection happened so quickly. When I asked, the student responded, "Well, we didn't talk about school." They simply had casual conversation not related to school. Prior to that weekend, the majority of their discussions centered on the teacher reminding and coercing him about his missing homework and inappropriate behavior.

I did not give it much further thought until the teacher came to me to tell me about the improvement that she was seeing in this student, a dramatic improvement in work output and behavior. The teacher was somewhat surprised when she realized that her class was the only one where the student showed improvement. I wish I could tell you that these changes were long term and generalized to the other subject areas, but this was not the case. The student's academic progress deteriorated after time, but his behavior improved immensely in that classroom for the duration of the school year.

Does this mean that all teachers should spend a weekend with their students with behavior problems? No, but the lesson to be learned is that students, especially difficult ones, often need to feel connected before improvements will be seen in behavior and academics. The natural tendency to focus the conversations with the students on what they are lacking does not build the relationship and can make matters worse. Mostly out of good intentions we tend to coerce, remind, and lecture students about what they should be doing. This rarely leads to improvement, especially with difficult students. Most difficult students have heard these types of lectures many times before. Ask yourself if one more time is going to make a difference.

Difficult students often assume their teachers do not like them, sometimes for good reason and sometimes irrationally. Research suggests that teachers unknowingly may treat difficult students differently by giving them less wait time to answer, more criticism, and less praise. They may call on them less frequently, demand less from them, seat them far away, and acknowledge positive behavior less often (Brophy & Good, 2000). An interview study of school dropouts found that only a small minority of them could name an adult at school they would consider a friend (Burns, 1996). It is usually the behavior of difficult children, not the children themselves, that we dislike. It is important to make sure that these students know that you like and care for them and not to assume that they know.

TIME CONSTRAINTS

Most teachers want to build positive relationships with students. Many chose a career in teaching because they care about students and want to make a positive difference. One of the biggest barriers to building relationships is time. Teachers are already overloaded with curricular demands, and in an effort to increase our students test scores we have increased curricular goals. When time is constrained, relationship building is often sacrificed. A central tenet of the relationship-driven approach is that we view relationship building as a complement to academic performance rather than as a competitor with academic goals. Despite time and curricular constraints, some teachers are still able to create positive and personal relationships by taking advantage of each interaction that they have with students.

Taking Advantage of Every Interaction

The relationship-driven teacher views all interactions with students as opportunities to strengthen the teacher-student relationship, including interactions involving disciplinary or corrective interactions. They use the first few or last few minutes of class, time between classes, tutorials, lunchtime, individual conferencing during independent work, after-school time, and sporting events to practice relationship building. Some teachers are even able to build relationships when they are managing behavior. Not only is each interaction significant to the individual student, but also the other students are observing the nature and tone of these interactions. If we yell, use harsh words, shame, degrade, or embarrass one student, all the students are affected. If you had a brother and sister growing up, how did you feel when they were punished? Usually, unless they were being punished for something that they did to you, you felt bad or scared. I can remember feeling scared and protective of my older brothers when my father was disciplining them. The point is that all students are affected by the treatment of one. If one or a few adults treat students overly harsh, it can have a negative effect on the whole school climate.

The positive side of the process of valuing all interactions is that it shows us that maybe we have more time than we think to build relationships with students. How many interactions do you think you have with each of your students? Obviously this varies across grade levels, but over the course of a year the number is fairly substantial. If we seek to take advantage of every interaction we can build a strong bond.

Most experts agree that to prevent misbehavior and maintain a positive climate there should be three to five positive interactions for every negative interaction in the classroom (Sprick et al., 1998). In other words, for every time that you have a negative or corrective interaction (a consequence is given) with a student or class, you should have three to five positive interactions. A positive interaction can be one where you recognize appropriate behavior in the student or class by giving them attention when they are behaving appropriately. A teacher can inadvertently increase negative behavior by paying attention to students more when they are misbehaving than when they are behaving appropriately.

Making Time for Positive Interactions

We owe it to our students to make time for building personal and positive relationships. Allocating this time is one of the components of safe and responsive schools (Dwyer et al., 1998). How the time is used is also an important variable. If schools set aside time for relationship building and it is used for tasks such as makeup work or study halls, then the benefits are lost.

Some schools have allocated more time for relationship building by using alternative scheduling (e.g., block scheduling), mentoring, advisory, and school-within-a-school frameworks. Ludwig and Mentley (1997) use an interesting relationship-building technique. One day a week the school hires a substitute teacher. Teachers choose a time during the day when the substitute teaches their classes, allowing them to have one-on-one time to meet with a student.

Looping is another emerging practice. Looping involves a child remaining with the same teacher for more than 1 year. For example, a teacher begins with a group of kindergartners and has these same students the following year as first graders or even again as second graders. The next year that teacher starts again with another group of kindergartners. Unfortunately, students in middle and high school have even less time to bond with adults, even though the need for time and relationships is equally important for this age group. Close relationships are even more important for at-risk middle and secondary school students (Lynch & Cicchetti, 1997).

Pianta (1999) recommends that schools maximize the time each student has with a single adult. He advocates for lower teacher-student ratios and more time to develop teacher-student relationships. He also makes an interesting point about students who receive pull-out services at school, such as students with a disability and high-risk students: These students may be pulled out up to five or six times per day for remediation with different adults, a practice that can be hurtful, especially for students with a high need for relationship stability. Schools may need to reduce the number of teachers the student interacts with to create time to build a healthy bond.

The next section addresses the distinction between positive and personal relationships and the importance of both.

POSITIVE AND PERSONAL RELATIONSHIPS

Relationship-driven teachers continually strive to build positive and personal relationships with their students. These teachers understand that having positive and personal connections with students is the best way to prevent misbehavior and increase motivation because students cooperate and work harder for teachers they love. Both a positive and personal relationship is important. It is possible to have a positive relationship without it being personal, but not vice versa. Many teachers have positive rapport with students, but fewer have personal relationships. A positive teacher-student relationship can often simply mean the absence of negative exchanges, whereas a personal relationship involves a deeper connection between teacher and student, one where there is mutual knowledge of both the teacher's and the student's interests, hopes, aspirations, and family life.

In interviewing teachers rated by peers, students, and administrators as having positive relationships with students, a number of themes emerged. First, these teachers seem to have an ability to find the right amount of self-disclosure, so the students see them as genuine. Second, they place a tremendous amount of emphasis on mutual respect, and they credit this respect for their success in making positive connections. Last, they have an uncanny ability for finding the right balance between being firm, fair, and friendly. When you ask students to describe teachers they feel connected to, they make statements such as the teacher "listens to me," "sees me as important," "talks with me," and "makes learning fun."

Norton (1995) talks about the importance of deep and personal relationships with students. He states that students long for the teacher to recognize them in such a way that makes them feel like an important person. In his interviews with teachers he found that the critical component that teachers point to in determining whether a positive and personal relationship will be formed is the student's inquisitiveness about the subject matter. Students who have a heightened interest, who are motivated, and who seek information related to the subject matter are more likely to develop a connection with the teacher. According to the author, these types of students make up only about 20% of the classroom. He encourages teachers to make more of an investment in students' whole lives as opposed to just their academic lives. Would you characterize your relationships with your students as both positive and personal?

Personal and Meaningful Dialogue

One way to develop personal and positive relationships with students is by engaging them in personal and meaningful dialogue. Most, if not all, students desire to be an important person to their teacher. When we talk with students about who they are, we communicate a caring message, one that makes students feel important and cared for. When we talk and listen, we send the message to the student that they are important and matter to us. Ideally this communication involves personal and nonacademic issues as well as academic issues, and it involves asking students about their interests, goals, aspirations, likes and dislikes, family, culture, and so on. Most students are open and willing to discuss these things with their teachers. One history teacher I observed builds relationships with his students by attending to and remembering the likes and dislikes of each of his students (favorite and least favorite sports, historical, political figure, etc.) and integrating this information into both academic and nonacademic discussions. He masterfully weaves his knowledge of the students' interests into the subject matter of history.

Students wonder about the personal lives of their teachers. Students love to hear about what teachers do on the weekends, funny stories about things that happen to them, or information about their families. Students want and need to know about the teacher; they need to know that you are a person with a life outside of school.

Teachers need to find a balance of revealing personal information about themselves and inquiring about the personal lives of students. We also can use too much self-disclosure, which might cause us to lose the respect of students. If a student revealed very personal issues in front of the entire class, you might tell the student in a subtle way that class is not the appropriate place for such disclosure. In a similar vein, we cannot use our students as a support group. Under no circumstances should we talk negatively about another colleague in front of students. When this happens, both your authority and the authority of other adults are undermined.

Many of us have our own style of relating and connecting to students. For teachers who wish to improve in this area, I usually recommend that they start by targeting one student and approach the student at an appropriate time, using a social starter such as "I notice you are interested in sports" or "You seem to really enjoy music." These two starters, "I notice . . . " and "You seem to . . . " are effective at beginning the process of meaningful dialogue. Cummings (2000) recommends a strategy of determining how many students you will have to initiate conversation with to have talked to everyone by the end of the week. For example, you would have to initiate six conversations per day with a class of 30 students to be able to converse will all students in one week. Another interesting strategy that she recommends is to require a ticket to leave the classroom. This ticket is the answer to a question that is written on the board. Questions on the board can be specific or open ended and can inquire about student perceptions of the class or lesson, what they would like to know more about, or their wishes or feelings.

RELATIONSHIP BUILDERS AND BARRIERS

Sometimes our behavior puts distance or a wedge between our students and us. Nelsen, Lott, and Glenn (2000) discuss what they call the five barriers and builders. The barriers undermine self-confidence and hurt trust, and the builders do the opposite. The barriers include assuming, rescuing or explaining, directing, expecting, and adultisms. The builders include checking, exploring, encouraging/inviting, celebrating, and respecting. The authors state that if all we do is reduce or eliminate the use of the barriers, we will experience a substantial improvement in all our relationships with children. The reader is directed to Nelsen et al. (2000) for in-depth coverage of the barriers and builders. A brief description of each barrier and builder follows:

* *Assuming.* In this barrier we assume how students will respond, think, and feel. For example, when we communicate with nagging and frequent reminders, we are assuming that students cannot change or that we know in advance how they will respond. It is discouraging to always be judged by past behavior. When we do this we are inadvertently setting low expectations for our students. Isn't it sometimes frustrating when someone reminds you of something that you are already prepared for? Or when someone does not tell you something because they assume you will react in a certain way? When tempted to assume or remind a student, it is better to use checking instead.

- *Checking.* We check by asking what students already know, by questioning and experimenting. Instead of saying, "Don't forget your money and permission slip for the field trip," we could use a checking builder and say, "What do we need to have before we go on the field trip?" Instead of saying, "Students, when we walk in the hallway, we keep our hands to ourselves and our voices quiet," we could say, "Students, what do we need to remember when walking in the hallway?" Instead of assuming that an intervention will not work with particular students, experiment and check to see if it might.

- *Rescuing or explaining.* In this barrier we rescue when we are too quick to solve, explain, or help our students. We do this when we tell our students what, why, and how something happened. A rescuing statement might be "This happened because . . . and it can be fixed if next time . . ." We struggle immensely with this barrier because of our desire to help and our ability to explain. However, we build problem-solving skills when we use exploring, instead of rescuing, and let students discover some of their own explanations and solutions.

- *Exploring.* We take the time to let the student discover what, why, and how in exploring. We use this builder when we ask a student to reflect on their experiences. By asking questions about how they view a situation, why it happened, and how it could be prevented next time, we communicate a message of capability to them. We are able to increase student problem-solving ability by asking students what could they do differently to prevent the same result. An excellent exploring question is "How might you go about solving this problem the next time." In the context of small-group work, we could ask, "How do you think your group cooperated with each other?" or "What happened in your group that influenced your project?" When exploring, be careful of the "why" questions, which can elicit defensiveness when used after a mistake or misbehavior; asking "why" is more effective when exploring intellectual cause and effect.

- *Directing.* In this barrier we boss or tell a student what needs to be done and how it needs to be done. When adults frequently dictate exactly what, how, when, and with whom to students, the students may not gain needed cooperation and independence skills. As adults when someone tells us exactly how to do something that we already know how to do, we can get frustrated and resentful. The same is true for our students. When we direct often, we communicate to students "I have a better way." Even if this is true, students sometimes need to learn to plan and experience the consequences on their own. The more controlling and directing we are with our students, the more rebellious they may be in return. It is important to be clear in your expectations for students, but too much direction can be a barrier in relationships with others.

- *Encouraging/Inviting.* Students are oftentimes more willing to cooperate when they are invited to contribute rather than told to contribute. An inviting teacher might say, "Class, I really need your help today to keep the room clean" or "Class, I would really appreciate it if you do your best work on this since we are going to hang our projects up in the hallway." Using inviting starter statements such as "Would you consider . . . ?" or "I would appreciate it if . . . " or "It would be very helpful if . . . " encourage students to cooperate and build the teacher-student relationship.

- *Expecting.* In this barrier, we criticize students, or point out what our students did not do right, and fail to acknowledge their successes or steps in the direction of success. This barrier is typically used when a teacher extends a compliment and attaches the word *but* at the end. We need to set high expectations for our students without continually noting when students fall short of these expectations, a practice that hurts relationships with our students.

- *Celebrations.* In this builder, we recognize successive approximations or increments in the direction of the desired expectation. For example, saying "Johnny, you are starting to look over your writing and put periods at the end of sentences" is better than saying, "Johnny, you forgot to put periods on some of these sentences." If necessary, at a later time you could address the mistakes. This communicates to the students that you do notice their successes and not just their failures.

- *Adultisms.* In this barrier we give messages to students that they should behave, think, and feel as we do. Examples of adultisms are "How come you never . . . ? How many times do I have to tell you . . . ? When will you ever learn? Don't you realize . . . ?" Adultisms frequently contain the word *should*.

- *Respecting.* In this builder, instead of expecting students to have our wisdom and view things the way we do, we explore how they view things and discuss the differences. Glenn and Nelsen (1989) state, "It is destructive to expect them to see what we see rather than exploring what they see and comparing notes" (p. 93). They suggest asking questions such as "What was your understanding of that?" or "How many of you became aware of this?"

Glasser (1998) contends that when we are faced with people or students who are not doing what we want them to do, we often resort to coercion, nagging, bossing, manipulating, punishing, rewarding, criticizing, blaming, and complaining. All of which, similar to the barriers explained previously, hurt relationships and are ineffective in the long term. Glasser suggests that we replace this tendency with ways in which we naturally interact with our long-term friends: We choose to care, listen, support, negotiate, encourage, befriend, trust, accept, welcome, and esteem. When teachers start to replace barriers with builders not only do their relationships with students improve, but they also report feeling better about themselves at the end of the day.

We should consider using more builders and reducing the barriers in our relationships. Does this mean that we should treat our students like we treat our friends? In some ways the answer to this question is yes. However, students need limits, structure, and consistency as well as strong and personal relationships with their teachers. This structure actually enhances their sense of trust, security, and respect for the teacher. In a relationship-driven classroom, the teacher strives for a balance of being firm, fair, and friendly. These concepts are adapted from Wubbolding's (1999) work on establishing trusting relationships with clients in counseling, coaching, and managing, but they are applicable to educators as well.

BALANCING FIRM, FAIR, AND FRIENDLY

In classrooms where frequent misbehavior and limit testing is the norm, it is usually the result of the teacher not striking a balance in the areas of being firm, fair, and friendly. For example, problems are likely to result in a class that has an abundance of friendliness but fails to have enough fairness and firmness. Similarly, problems are inevitable when the teacher is very firm and fair but lacks friendliness. Effective teachers are able to strike a delicate balance between the three.

On Being Firm

Being firm requires consistency, assertiveness, and clear expectations. Consistency teaches students that there are predictable outcomes to behavior. A teacher who lacks firmness often fails to respond consistently to the misbehavior in the classroom, fails to follow through with predetermined consequences, and may deliver consequences for the same misbehavior in some instances but not in others (Knoff, 2001).

Students frequently test the limits in an inconsistent classroom. Simply stated, without consistency teachers and rules lose credibility. Some teachers make the mistake of not backing up their words with actions. The students quickly learn that the words from this teacher have little power behind them. The students learn that they can ignore the first, second, or even third request before the teacher gets angry, states an ultimatum, or delivers a consequence. When teachers finally do give a consequence, the students claim that it is unfair because the same misbehavior doesn't always receive a consequence, and in some cases other students displayed similar behaviors and did not receive any consequence.

Another key component of consistency is monitoring. Oftentimes an inconsistent teacher will give a request and then get distracted and fail to monitor whether the students are complying within a reasonable time limit. In this scenario, students quickly learn to delay compliance. Consistency can be the difference between an effective classroom and a chaotic one. If you notice that you must deliver numerous reminders to students or students are not complying with your requests within a reasonable time limit, consistency might be to blame. Firm teachers set clear expectations and limits, check for understanding, monitor student compliance, and consistently follow through with consequences as necessary. We should routinely ask ourselves if we are using adequate amounts of firmness.

On Being Fair

Fairness requires being impartial and resisting the tendency to favor certain types of individuals or groups over others. As mentioned previously, a lack of consistency can increase a student's perception of inequity. In many classrooms, difficult students are punished for behaviors that are not dissimilar to the behavior of others (Brophy & Good, 2000). Partiality, taken to a more extreme level, was mentioned as a potential causal factor in the Columbine High School shooting (U.S. Secret Service Safe School Initiative, 2000). The students who committed the shooting resented what they perceived as a double standard between the treatment of athletes and nonathletes, especially in the severity of consequences they received for misbehavior.

Another common example seen in classrooms is the assumption that a certain student is to blame for conflicts. For example, Bill, a sixth grader, was often argumentative and sometimes failed to accept responsibility for his behavior. Whenever a conflict arose between him and another student, the teacher often assumed that Bill was to blame. When this situation was explored by the principal and support staff, it was determined that Bill was being bullied, teased, and excluded by the other students, most of the time behind the teacher's back.

Assumptions like this can lead to an escalation of conflict and a feeling of being misunderstood and unfairly judged by past behavior. When we judge a student based on past behavior, we send a discouraging message, and we are not being fair when we hold students accountable long after an incident or continually remind them of past misbehavior. To the extent that it is possible, students need to start the next day with a clean slate. We should ask ourselves, "Do I respect students and treat them fairly even if I may not always like their behavior?"

On Being Friendly

Friendliness involves a myriad of specific and general temperamental and personality variables, but, generally speaking, friendly teachers speak with a calm tone of voice, do not take misbehavior personally, are not overly task driven, show interest in the whole student, are empathetic and courteous, and have a sense of humor. Friendliness in teacher-student relationships is often taboo because it requires the adult to relinquish some control. This taboo is found in the foolish age-old advice given to new teachers: "Don't smile until Christmas."

Ask yourself whom you would rather work for: a friendly and caring person or an unfriendly and uncaring person? Would you rather do quality work for someone who uses a rude, mean, or sarcastic tone of voice or someone who uses a calm and courteous voice? We should thoroughly and continually self-evaluate our friendliness with students. We could self-evaluate most of our character traits by asking ourselves, "How would my students describe me most of the time?" I encourage teachers to think about how they would like a boss or significant other to let them know they had made a mistake. After reflecting on how you would like to be treated, ask yourself how closely this is alike or dissimilar to how you treat your students when they make a mistake. Do our students deserve to be treated as we would like to be treated under similar circumstances? We should routinely ask ourselves if we are using adequate amounts of friendliness in the classroom.

In summary, the relationship-driven teacher strives to prevent misbehavior, increase achievement and motivation, and enhance resilience by developing positive and personal connections with students. They do this by using time wisely, using more relationship builders than barriers, and by finding a balance between being firm, fair, and friendly.

SUMMARY OF MAIN POINTS

- Positive teacher-student relationships have substantial research support and have been shown to increase academic achievement and motivation, reduce school dropout and substance abuse, and prevent emotional problems.

- When teachers engage in meaningful dialogue and talk with students about their interests, hopes, families, opinions— and when they appropriately disclose personal information about their own lives—it sends a strong message of caring and lets the student know that he or she is important.

- A relationship-driven teacher takes advantage of every interaction with students to build positive and personal relationships. The relationship-driven teacher gives more attention to positive behavior than to negative behavior and strives to have three to five positive interactions to every one negative interaction with the class or a particular student.

- Relationship barriers hurt relationships and include choosing to nag, remind, rescue, lecture, punish, coerce, boss, criticize, assume, and manipulate.

- Relationship builders help relationships and include choosing to listen, check for understanding, explore the student's perception of the situation, befriend, care, negotiate, esteem, invite, encourage, and celebrate successes.

- Trust is fostered in the classroom when the teacher strikes a delicate balance between being firm, fair, and friendly.

QUESTIONS FOR DISCUSSION AND SELF-EVALUATION

1. What are some ways that you currently foster positive and personal relationships with your students?

2. What are some possible reasons why teachers feel better about themselves and less stressed when they replace relationship barriers with builders with their students?

3. What strategies can you use to ensure that the ratio of positive interactions in your classroom is much greater (i.e., 4:1) in comparison to negative interactions?

4. Do your students leave your classroom knowing you as a person or just as a teacher?

5. What are some barriers to prioritizing teacher-student relationships in your classroom and school?

ACTION PLAN

As a result of something that I learned in this chapter I plan to (be specific in your answer):

_____

_____

_____

RECOMMENDED RESOURCES

Brendtro, L., Brokenleg, M., & Van Bockern, S. (1998). *Reclaiming youth at risk: Our hope for the future.* Bloomington, IN: National Educational Service. This book highlights the importance of relationships and social bonds in interventions for challenging youth and describes the importance of establishing or reclaiming a safe environment for our at-risk youth.

Glasser, W. (1998). *Choice theory: A new psychology of personal freedom.* New York: HarperCollins. This book addresses the importance of relationships in psychotherapy, home, school, and work.

Nelsen, J., Lott, L., & Glenn, S. (2000). *Positive discipline in the classroom: Developing mutual respect, cooperation, and responsibility in your classroom.* Roseville, CA: Prima Publishing. This book discusses relationship builders and barriers and provides numerous positive strategies to improve classroom behavior and student responsibility.

Pianta, R. (1999). *Enhancing relationships between children and teachers.* Washington, DC: American Psychological Association. This book is written in a scientific and scholarly style but provides some excellent insights into teacher-student relationships.

CHAPTER FIVE

Teaching and Modeling Social-Emotional Skills

"If the teacher does not model what is being taught, then something else is being taught."

—Author Unknown

CHAPTER OBJECTIVES

In this chapter the reader will learn:

- Social-emotional skills that are related to resilience, effective behavior, and academic achievement
- Examples of how to integrate social-emotional skills into the classroom and curriculum
- Resources of proven effective programs for teaching social-emotional skills

THE IMPORTANCE OF TEACHING SOCIAL-EMOTIONAL SKILLS

A relationship-driven teacher understands the value of social and emotional skills and their positive impact on students' learning, behavior, and quality of life. Teaching social-emotional skills to all students is prevention rather than reaction oriented. When students possess social-emotional skills, they are more likely to engage in learning and less likely to misbehave. Doll (1994) estimates that in the typical elementary school of 1,000 students, the following problems exist:

- Forty-five to 50 students have conduct disorders.
- Twenty-five to 65 students have attention deficit disorder.
- One hundred eighty to 210 students have anxiety disorders.
- Six to 14 students are depressed.
- One hundred ten students are being physically abused.

In secondary schools the numbers show an increase in substance abuse, depression, eating disorders, and suicidal ideation (thoughts). Although these numbers are just estimates, they reveal a picture of the clientele we are asked to educate. Our students have much on their minds besides academics. It is estimated that 25% of children between the ages of 10 and 17 are engaged in many high-risk behaviors and are considered extremely vulnerable. In addition, another 25% are considered moderately vulnerable (Zins, Elias, Greenberg, & Kline Pruett, 2000). This, paired with the estimate that less than 25% of children who have significant mental health problems receive appropriate services, highlights the need for teaching social-emotional competence (Tuma, 1989).

In addition, neuroscience is finding that our emotions play a critical role in memory and learning (LeDoux, 1998). The social-emotional competencies that are often cited as important in learning and resilience are social skills, problem solving, self-control, self-efficacy, and optimism. These social-emotional skills are protective factors, or assets, that have been shown to increase a child's

Figure 5.1 Internal Protective Factors/Social-Emotional Skills

Relationship and Social Skills

➢ Self-awareness
➢ Empathy
➢ Communication skills
➢ Conflict resolution skills

Problem-Solving Skills

➢ Ability to generate alternate solutions
➢ Abstract and flexible thought

Self-Control

➢ Delay of gratification
➢ Persistence
➢ Thinking of consequences before act

Self-Efficacy

➢ Belief that one can influence one's own life
➢ Belief that one can accomplish tasks

Optimism

➢ Hope for better future
➢ Goal directed
➢ Nonnegative explanation of events

ability to cope with adversity or increase resilience. Figure 5.1 summarizes these skills.

Social-emotional skills can either impede or enhance learning and are critical factors in work and life success (Goleman, 1995). Students may be able to learn without some of these social-emotional skills, but when we neglect these components, we fail to tap students' full potential. According to Zins et al. (2000) schools have found that when they systematically focus on social-emotional skills, academic achievement increases, behavior problems decrease, and the quality of relationships surrounding each student improves. These skills can be infused into both the curriculum and the classroom management system or taught separately from the academic curriculum.

SOCIAL-EMOTIONAL LEARNING PROGRAMS

A variety of programs exist to help teachers incorporate social-emotional learning into the curriculum. The Emotional Literacy Project, 6 Seconds, Enchanted Innertainment, and the Collaborative for Academic, Social, and Emotional Learning (CASEL) are great sources for the reader who is interested in social-emotional learning, and all can be accessed through the World Wide Web. CASEL (www.casel.org) conducts research and disseminates information on social-emotional learning. They advocate for instructional practices that use a variety of intelligences, repeated rehearsal of social-emotional skills, and prompting and cueing the use of social-emotional skills throughout the school day in natural contexts. CASEL states that integration of social-emotional learning into the general curriculum, as opposed to teaching the skills separately, improves both academics and behavior. In other words, social-emotional learning complements academic learning (Zins et al., 1998). In addition, students gain confidence from practicing acquired social-emotional skills and receiving positive feedback. CASEL recommends that social-emotional learning be a part of the entire school curriculum, not simply a fragmented add-on.

MODELING

In addition to direct teaching, teachers can also model the skills for students, which is a very effective indirect form of teaching. When we do not model the same behaviors that we ask of our students, they are unlikely to buy in to their importance. Children are particularly astute at detecting adult hypocrisy or an inability to walk the talk. I was involved in a campaign to prioritize and improve sportsmanship of student athletes. We required coaches to teach their athletes appropriate sportsmanship. During our sportsmanship campaign we realized we had been remiss to the power of negative modeling. At a home football game a parent confronted one of the coaches and a fistfight ensued. The following year at an away indoor soccer match the adult fans came out of the stands and attacked the high school and middle school players, and that same year a parent strangled his child on the sidelines of a basketball game. These incidents were in addition to the usual numerous examples of adults yelling and berating the referees. When the message doesn't match the behavioral modeling, failure is inevitable.

Conflict management approaches can help teachers model social-emotional skills. Conflict management is an effective approach or set of approaches that teach skills that preserve relationships. A teacher has many opportunities to model and teach conflict resolution skills when two or more students are in a conflict or when there is a teacher-student conflict, both of which come up often in the typical classroom. For example, when a student repeatedly disrupts a lesson, an obvious conflict exists between the teacher and student. If the teacher responds hastily and angrily, poor conflict resolution skills and poor self-control skills are modeled. A more effective response would be for the teacher to respond calmly and state, "It is difficult to teach and learn when you are choosing to disrupt. What other behaviors might you choose so everyone's learning is not hurt?" In other words, the teacher models conflict resolution skills by attempting to talk to solve the problem.

When we confront our students angrily or harshly, we may also be modeling poor self-control. When confronted students' emotions and brain defenses increase in intensity, which makes it almost impossible to think carefully and critically. However, it is at these times that we want students to think, reflect, and plan for better behavior. The point here is that we need to be careful that we are modeling effective social-emotional skills to our students. What message does your behavior send to your students? How do you confront student misbehavior when you are frustrated? Is your response to anger and frustration what you would like to see in your students?

Relationship-driven teachers realize the power of modeling and examine how they model the social-emotional competencies that they want to see in their students. The rest of the chapter is devoted to the five protective factors or social-emotional skills that enhance learning, behavior, and resilience. Strategies that build each of the five skills and proven curricular materials are also reviewed.

RELATIONSHIP AND SOCIAL SKILLS

Social skills are often left up to chance in our classrooms. It is often assumed that students should or already do possess the necessary social skills and that they should learn these at home. The social skills considered most critical for student development are self-awareness, empathy, communication, and conflict resolution skills. These skills help students to build and maintain friendships and a sense of belonging. When students feel like they belong, they are in a better position to learn; when they feel like they do not belong, they often turn to misbehavior. Students who lack social skills are distracted from learning by the tremendous amount of energy they expend trying to fit in and manage social conflicts and teasing.

Social skill deficits are cited by teachers as the most frequent cause of classroom behavior problems (Brophy & Good, 2000). Yet we often fail to allocate ample time for instruction and training in prosocial skills. Instead of punishing students for not having adequate social skill, time might better be spent instructing, practicing, and recognizing prosocial behaviors.

Integrating Social Skills in the Classroom

Traditionally, teachers identify students with social skill deficits and refer them to a pull-out intervention or social skills group, which consists of students with similar deficits or problems meeting periodically to practice social skills. There are some advantages to classwide social skills training versus a pull-out approach. With a classwide approach, students are not removed from the classroom and curriculum, have more opportunities to see students with well-developed social skills model those skills, and are able to have the classroom teacher involved in the interventions (Merrell, 2002). In addition, the teacher is often in a unique position to integrate the social skills being taught into real situations that occur in the classroom or on the playground. Another advantage of the classwide approach is that all students—not just the most severe—receive the skills. The downside to pull-out programs is reduced self-esteem. Students in pull-out groups can be subject to ridicule. Many times students will learn social skills in a pull-out group only to continue to be rejected by students outside the group because many of these students are also lacking in social skills, especially empathy. When all students are involved, this problem is reduced.

The teacher can improve the social skills of the class by modeling, noticing, and discussing appropriate social skills. The most obvious way to build social skills is by integrating the skills into the existing curriculum. For example, analyzing social traits of historical figures or character traits within a story is one way to draw attention to social skills. After examining the different social skills or traits of the historical figures or characters in a story, students can choose which character they would select as a friend. Cummings (2000) recommends selecting reading materials that give rich examples of traits like self-discipline, problem solving, perseverance, and self-control. She recommends *The Book of Virtues* by William Bennett (1996) since literary selections are already organized into themes.

One interesting strategy, adapted from Sprick et al. (1998), is to incorporate social skills into the classroom by using a mystery social skill. At the beginning of the day or week the teacher writes an important social skill on a piece of paper and places it in an envelope. Students are told that the teacher will be watching for this mystery social skill, but they are not told what it is until the end of the day or week. Students who exhibit the behavior receive a treat at the end of the observation period. Teachers who use this system should vary the mystery behavior to ensure that every student earns a reward. This strategy is especially helpful as an extension when social skills lessons have already been taught in the classroom.

Role-Playing Techniques

Almost all social skills curricula include a role-playing component. Role-play allows the students to practice the skills by acting out the role or pretending. Role-play increases empathy—it gives students the chance to put themselves in the shoes of

Figure 5.2 Cognitive-Behavioral Instructional Model

Instruction and Demonstration

- Explain a skill in a detailed, step-by-step manner.
- Give detailed explanation of when to use the skill.
- Demonstrate how to perform the skill.

Role-Play or Rehearsal

- Give all students opportunities to practice the skill in a pretend scenario.

Feedback and Social Reinforcement

- Give supportive and constructive feedback about specific aspects of role play or practice and areas that need improvement.
- Give specific recommendations or provide a plan on how to improve.

Extended Practice

- Discuss ways to use the skill in common situations.
- Assign behavior homework to practice skill.

another, which is an underlying skill for most beginning and advanced social skills. In addition, it gives the students the opportunity to practice the social skill as opposed to just hearing someone else tell them how they should act.

Many social skills programs and other social-emotional competence-building programs use a cognitive-behavioral instructional model: instruction and demonstration, role-play, group feedback, reinforcement, rehearsal, and extended practice through behavioral homework assignments. The reader will notice that this model could also be used as an effective way to teach some academic skills. Figure 5.2 outlines this instructional approach. Figure 5.3 provides a general framework for most structured learning approaches to social skills training. To give the reader a better understanding of how social skills can be taught and practiced in the classroom, I next discuss conflict resolution, bully prevention, base groups, and the Stop and Think Social Skills Program. Self-awareness, or being aware of how our

Figure 5.3 Framework for Teaching Social Skills

- Establish the need for the new skill and increase motivation.
- Identify the skill components or subskills needed.
- Rehearse behaviors (i.e., role-play).
- Provide feedback about role-play.
- Encourage generalization through practice and cue use in real-world situations.

behavior influences others, is an important social skill. Strategies to build self-awareness will be covered in the self-control section coming up later in this chapter.

Conflict Resolution

Most social skills programs include conflict resolution skills. Conflict resolution training has numerous benefits to students and teachers, including assisting students in effectively solving conflicts, preventing the escalation of conflict into violence, preserving relationships, and increasing skills in listening, critical thinking, and problem solving. Students who are trained in conflict resolution skills are more likely to use problem solving to solve conflicts, instead of withdrawing or using violence (Johnson & Johnson, 1995). Johnson and Johnson cite their own research, which shows that training students in conflict resolution increases their academic performance as well. In addition, students who are resilient often have strong conflict resolution skills (Benard, 1995). There are numerous conflict resolution programs available, varying from classroom approaches to whole-school or districtwide comprehensive conflict management programs. Peer mediation, a popular form of conflict resolution, trains students to mediate conflicts of their peers.

A typical sequence for conflict resolution might include gathering information and describing the conflict, listening to and stating each person's point of view, brainstorming possible win-win solutions, negotiating or compromising, thinking about consequences of possible solutions, trying the best solution, and, if it doesn't work, trying another. Most approaches to conflict resolution teach students a sequence of steps to follow to reach a solution. Generally there are only three possible outcomes to conflict: lose-lose, win-lose, and win-win. A solution in conflict resolution terms is when both people win or get to a mutually satisfying solution—a win-win solution. A win-win solution does not necessarily mean that each party gets exactly what they want but that they get some of what they want. Getting to win-win solutions is the goal of most conflict resolutions programs and involves understanding conflict, mediation, negotiation, and consensus-seeking skills.

Mediation and Negotiation

When a third party is involved to assist in the conflict resolution process, it is called mediation. When the two parties are practicing conflict resolution without a mediator, it is called negotiation. The following are six steps to negotiation and mediation, adapted from Johnson and Johnson (1995):

1. *Agree to mediate or negotiate.* If a mediator is involved, his or her role and some ground rules are explained, and each person is asked if they are willing to participate in the process. If it is a negotiation, both people mutually agree to try to solve the problem.

2. *Gather points of view.* Each person describes what happened and his or her feelings, and then the students reverse roles and summarize the other person's description and feelings. This increases understanding of feelings and increases empathy.

3. *Focus on interests.* Each person states what they want and why, and then each person reverses and tells what the other person wants and why. Both people attempt to find commonalities in what they want.

4. *Create win-win options.* Brainstorm—without judging—a minimum of three possible solutions or as many solutions as can be developed.

5. *Evaluate options.* Students then decide if the options can be combined and if each one is fair, doable, and workable.

6. *Create an agreement.* A detailed plan of action or agreement is reached. Students state or write the agreed-upon plan and restate what they have agreed to do.

Group Problem Solving and Consensus

Another form of conflict resolution is group problem solving. Group problem solving is effective when a problem impacts many or all individuals in a group or classroom. The most important part of group problem solving is consensus, which is also called consensus decision making. It is important to make the distinction between voting and consensus. When a class or group of students has a conflict or a decision to make, they often vote. In a vote there are always winners and losers; however, in a consensus all participants examine different viewpoints and arrive at an agreement that is best for the entire class. Each participant agrees on what he or she will accept or live with. The key to consensus decision making is making sure students understand that they might not get their favorite or first choice but will have a voice in what is best for the whole group.

The most effective conflict resolution programs involve all students and all adults in the training, as opposed to a select group. In addition, it is important that adults model the skills each day when conflicts and behavior problems arise in the classroom. Some classrooms or schools train all students in the process of conflict resolution and then rotate which students will act as mediators throughout the year. Other programs train all students and staff and practice the strategies within the curriculum without the use of student mediators. Even young students can learn the concepts and processes of conflict resolution. When students have practiced the concepts of conflict resolution, they can usually go through the process without adult assistance or with only minor adult assistance and prompting. An excellent source for more information on conflict resolution is *Creating the Peaceable School* (Bodine, Crawford, & Schrumpf, 1994). Dealing with bullying and teasing is in an important social skill that is related to conflict resolution.

Bullying

Bullying behaviors are prevalent in our schools and include behaviors such as physical, social, verbal, and written aggression; intimidation; and sexual and racial harassment. Social aggression involves spreading rumors, gossiping, excluding others from a group, and social rejection. Olweus (1999) defines bullying as exposure of a person, repeatedly and over time, to negative actions on the part of one or more persons. Bullying usually involves an imbalance of power—physically, socially, psychologically, or intellectually—that interferes with a person's self-defense abilities.

Ten to 15% of all children report being bullied regularly (Beane, 1999). One common myth about bullying is that it only affects the victims. According to Beane, bullying affects everyone since many students are anxious and wondering who will be next. The U.S. Secret Service (2000), in its study of school shootings, found that in almost 70% of the cases the attackers felt persecuted, bullied, threatened, or injured by others prior to the incident. The authors concluded, "A number of attackers had experienced bullying and harassment that was long standing and severe. In these cases, the experience of bullying appeared to play a major role in motivating the attack at school" (p. 7).

To understand and prevent bullying we must have an understanding of both victims and bullies. The biggest targets of bullies are not necessarily students who look different. The biggest targets are students who are passive, anxious, insecure, cry easily, and lack social skills (Bonds & Stoker, 2000). Bullies, on the other hand, tend to lack empathy and guilt, have a small group of friends who admire or secretly fear their behavior, have unrealistically high self-esteem, and often have a parent who models aggression.

The Role of Teachers in Dealing With Bullying

The teacher is a critical figure in recognizing and intervening in cases of bullying and teasing. The most effective way to intervene in cases of bullying is to calmly let the bully know what school or class rule was violated, what the consequences will be, and that you expect students to respect each other. You should also help the bully understand the feelings of the victim. If possible, consequences should include the bullies doing something positive or helpful for the school or for others. The teacher should be careful to avoid modeling bullying behavior when they deal with the bully. If we deal with bullies in a harsh or demeaning way, we may send the message that bullying is acceptable for adults but not for students. We can send a clear message about bullying without using bully tactics, such as threatening and intimidation.

In terms of bully prevention, teachers can discuss the facts about bullying, discuss student perspectives on bullying, teach friendship and conflict resolution skills, help all students feel accepted, encourage students to report instances of bullying, and intervene immediately when bullying is reported. Students can be encouraged to report bullying by telling them that if they do nothing about bullying, they are saying to the bully that it is acceptable. After discussing bullying with the class, the students could decide to designate their classroom as a bully-free classroom.

Schools that make supervision a priority, especially during unstructured times, such as transitions between classes, lunch, recess, and bus rides to and from school, experience less bullying. In addition, schools that send a message that bullying will not be tolerated, communicate consequences for these behaviors, and intervene in all bullying situations experience fewer bullying instances (Bonds & Stoker, 2000). Simply having consequences and stiffer penalties for bullying will not eliminate bullying since it often goes on without the knowledge of adults.

Bully Prevention Programs

Olweus (1999) has a documented bully prevention program that focuses on education for parents, teachers, and students; clear schoolwide rules against bullying; consequences for bullying and rewards for appropriate behavior; regular class meetings to discuss bullying and peer relationships; improved supervision of children during break periods; increased teacher involvement in creating a positive school climate; and individual meetings with bullies and victims or targets of bullying. This program requires the formation of a school bullying-prevention coordinating committee. This program has led to about a 50% reduction in bullying. Two other bully prevention programs are *The Bully Free Classroom* (Beane, 1999) and *Bully-Proofing Your School: A Comprehensive Approach for Middle Schools* (Bonds & Stoker, 2000).

Base Groups

Base groups are an excellent way to build social skills, improve student relationships, increase student belonging, and reduce student alienation. Base groups are formed toward the beginning of the school year, after the teacher has gotten to know the social characteristics of the students, and lasts until the end of the school year. The groups initially consist of two or three students, with room for a maximum of four if a new student comes into the classroom. Norton (1995) describes the purposes and responsibilities of the base group:

- To build social skills of the members
- To act as a support group for the members
- To assist other members in problem solving
- To act as study buddies or peer tutors for other members of the group
- To welcome new students in the group and assist in teaching classroom rules, routines, and expectations
- To discuss current affairs and school and classroom concerns
- To develop action plans based on class learning

The primary role of the base group is to learn and practice social skills. In addition, students can get into base groups to discuss and role-play after a whole-class lesson on a social skill. A teacher may use base groups in a similar fashion to support students: If a student is having difficulty with a social skill, the teacher suggests that the student enlist the help of the base group.

Norton (1995) recommends that before beginning base groups with students, you discuss the functions, expectations, and benefits of the groups. The two rules for the groups are maintaining confidentiality (except when students report abuse to the group) and refraining from changing or switching groups. He stresses that students must see the benefits and must sense the enthusiasm of the teacher toward the groups. Once the groups are formed, they should start with group trust and cohesion-building activities. These trust-building activities can involve learning the names, hobbies, and favorites of your teammates and developing team names, T-shirts, colors, and handshakes to build team identity and unity. These activities can take place as often as necessary, but Norton recommends that they take place three times per week for 1 month. Kagan (1994) calls these activities team builders and provides numerous strategies to build team identity, mutual support, valuing of differences, and synergy. Once trust and cohesion are established, the teacher or any of the group members can call on the group for help.

The Stop and Think Social Skills Program

One very promising program for preschool through Grade 8 is called The Stop and Think Social Skills Program (Knoff, 2001). This program has empirical support and the endorsement as a National Model Prevention Program by the U.S. Department of Health and Human Services. The program has impressive results, including decreased student discipline referrals and suspension and expulsions, improvements in social interactions, and increased on-task behavior and academic performance. The program uses a common learning component, such as those in Figures 5.2 and 5.3. In addition, five steps are used when teaching any social skill:

1. Stop and think!

2. Are you going to make a good choice or a bad choice?

3. What are your choices or steps?

4. Just do it!

5. Good job!

This program organizes social skills into four areas:

1. Survival skills (e.g., listening, following directions, ignoring distractions, using nice or brave talk, rewarding yourself)

2. Interpersonal skills (e.g., sharing, asking for permission, joining an activity, waiting for your turn)

3. Problem-solving skills (e.g., asking for help, apologizing, accepting consequences, deciding what to do)

4. Conflict resolution skills (e.g., dealing with teasing, losing, accusations, being left out, peer pressure)

A typical lesson would involve teaching the steps of the social skill, modeling the steps with a provided script, role-playing the steps and script, giving performance feedback, and having the students use the skill as many times as possible in natural settings during the day and in different situations. A manual and repro-ducible social skills cue cards for posting and student distribution are available. The manual also contains a useful template to plan social skills training for the entire school year.

Out of the five social-emotional skills discussed in this chapter, social skill training is probably the most important. Without adequate social skills students are not able to develop and maintain relationships. When students are not able to develop satisfying relationships, they may act out or display negative attention-getting behaviors. Students who have experienced a history of unsatisfactory relationships may be at risk for serious and destructive behaviors.

Social Skills Curricula

A variety of other social skills curricula are available, including the following:

- *Skillstreaming the Elementary School Child: New Strategies and Perspectives for Teaching Social Skills* (1997), by E. McGinnis and A. Goldstein. Champaign, IL: Research Press; *Skillstreaming the Adolescent* (1980), by A. Goldstein, R. Sprafkin, N. Gershaw, and P. Klein. Champaign, IL: Research Press. Separate programs for elementary school children and adolescents.
- *The Walker Social Skills Curriculum-ACCEPTS Program* (1983), by H. Walker, et al. Austin, TX: PRO-ED. Grades K–6.
- *The Stop & Think Social Skills Program* (2001), by H. Knoff. Longmont, CO: Sopris West. Preschool–Grade 8.
- *Tribes: A New Way of Learning and Being Together* (1995), by J. Gibbs. Windsor, CA: CenterSource Systems.

PROBLEM SOLVING

Students who lack problem-solving skills may have difficulty with maintaining friendships, academics, and critical and independent thinking. Problem solving, or the ability to generate alternate solutions to problems, is not only a protective factor but also an important academic and curricular goal. Of all the protective factors and social skills, problem solving is the most teacher friendly because it is already a requirement in most academic curricula.

Problem solving and critical thinking should be key components of classroom management as well, requiring students to problem solve routinely by developing a plan for improvement when they misbehave. Problem solving can be integrated easily into reading, math, history, and science. Problem solving can be taught by asking students questions such as, for example in history, "How did the person handle the situation?" and "Can you think of another way they could have handled the situation that would have been better?"

One obstacle to building problem-solving skills is the tendency for adults to solve or explain the problem for the child. Our role of compassionate helper actually can be a hindrance to children developing solutions to problems. Instead of rushing in, teachers can assist in the development of problem solving by asking facilitative questions and helping students evaluate the consequences of their proposed solutions. One of the best strategies to improve problem solving is self-instructional problem solving. In this method, the teacher approaches a problem to be solved with a series of questions he or she asks aloud. In simplified terms, the teacher just talks his or her way through each step in the problem-solving sequence. The students are taught to ask the same questions to solve problems, beginning with repeating the steps aloud as they solve problems, gradually moving toward writing the steps down and finally to subvocalizing (stating quietly to oneself) the steps. The typical questions in a self-instructional academic problem-solving sequence might be the following:

1. What is the problem asking?

2. Does this problem look like problems I have solved before?

3. What is the first step? Second step? Third?

4. Does this answer make sense?

The typical sequence in social problem solving might be as follows:

1. Problem recognition and identification

2. Generation of solutions (brainstorming)

3. Consequential thinking (What are the consequences of the potential solutions?)

4. Decision making (choose the best one)

5. Reviewing outcomes (If first choice doesn't work, choose another solution)

Promoting Alternative Thinking Strategies, or PATHS (Kusche & Greenberg, 1994), teaches 11 steps of interpersonal cognitive problem solving, which are summarized in Figure 5.4. The PATHS curriculum was developed for elementary students and is taught 3 days per week. The manual provides teachers with lessons, materials, and instructions for teaching interpersonal problem-solving skills, emotional literacy, self-control, and social competence. Some lesson examples include identifying and labeling feelings, interpreting social cues, problem solving, decision making, and reducing stress.

Shure (2001) developed the I Can Problem Solve (ICPS) training program, which targets six skills in his interpersonal cognitive problem-solving model: alternative solution thinking, consequential thinking, causal thinking, interpersonal sensitivity, means-end thinking, and perspective taking. The program also contains lessons that build sensitivity to other people's motivations for behavior and listening and awareness skills. The ICPS contains three separate volumes for preschool, kindergarten, and primary grades. The curriculum involves formal lessons, interaction in the classroom, and academic curriculum integration.

The goal of the program is for students to practice generating solutions to real-world problems, anticipating potential consequences, and planning sequenced steps toward an interpersonal goal. Teachers using the ICPS model communicate with students when there is a problem using what is called ICPS dialoguing. Teachers avoid telling, suggesting, or even explaining why a student should or should not try a particular strategy to solve the problem. Children are simply asked questions to help define the problem, understand the feelings of others, and guide consequential thinking (what might happen if . . .).

SELF-CONTROL

Students who lack self-control have difficulty attending to and persevering on academic tasks, following school rules, and

Figure 5.4   Interpersonal Cognitive Problem-Solving Steps in
PATHS

Stop

- Stop and think.
- Identify the problem.
- Identify the feeling.

Get Ready—What Could I Do?

- Decide on a goal.
- Generate alternative solutions.
- Evaluate possible consequences of solutions.
- Select the best solution.
- Plan the solution.

Go—Try My Best Plan

- Try the plan.

Evaluate—How Did I Do?

- Evaluate the outcome.
- Try another solution or reevaluate the goal.

---

maintaining friendships. Self-control, or the ability to regulate oneself and one's emotions, delay gratification, and think before acting, is critical for classroom and life success. One of the best strategies to improve self-control in the classroom is to provide predictability and consistency. Students learn to control themselves in environments where they have clear expectations for behavior and certain consequences consistently and predictably follow certain behaviors.

Self-control can also be enhanced by reminding or cueing students to stop and think or to self-monitor. Self-monitoring and self-management, also called self-recording, are strategies in which students learn to keep track of their own behavior. Some programs use a cue that signals students to evaluate what they are doing and to record this behavior. This facilitates the development of self-awareness. Students can be taught to self-record, self-correct, and possibly even self-reinforce when they are successful. An example of a self-monitoring strategy for a student with poor self-control (talking out in this example) might be as follows:

- Discuss the behavior to be measured with student. It is better to monitor a positive behavior (raising hand) than a negative behavior (talking out).

- Teach the student how to keep track or measure the behavior, such as asking the student to use a tally chart on his or her desk or notebook.

- The student keeps track and records number of times he or she raises a hand before speaking.

- The student and teacher set a goal, which may change as the program continues, and a review date.

- The student uses self-praise or self-reinforcement if the goal is attained.

- The teacher may also keep track of the behavior at first and later periodically to check and acknowledge reliability and accuracy for the student.

One of the goals is for the student to become more self-aware and accurate in self-tracking of behaviors. Self-monitoring, which can be taught to individual students or to entire classrooms, has an advantage over many interventions because it directly involves the student and is not overly demanding of teacher time. Self-monitoring strategies are discussed further in Chapter 7.

Anger management is related to self-control. Anger management usually involves teaching students to recognize physical cues that they are about to get angry, teaching them to breath or count to 10 to calm down, and teaching them to move out of the situation if necessary or communicate their feelings appropriately. Most anger control programs include strategies to improve social perspective taking (understand the motives of others), relaxation training, and generating as many alternative solutions as possible.

Self-Control Curricula

Some available self-control curricula include the following:

- Stop and Think Programs (1993), by P. C. Kendall and L. Braswell. In *Cognitive-Behavioral Therapy for Impulsive Children.* New York: Guilford Press.
- Anger Coping Program (1993), by J. Lochman, S. Dunn, and B. Klimes-Dougan. In "An Intervention and Consultation Model From a Social Cognitive Perspective: A Description of the Anger Coping Program," *School Psychology Review, 22*(3).
- Anger Control Training (1986), by E. L. Feindler and R. B. Ecton. In *Adolescent Anger Control: Cognitive-Behavioral Techniques.* Elmsford, NY: Pergamon Press.

SELF-EFFICACY

Students who lack self-efficacy struggle to see that success is within their means and may be prone to give up easily, be easily discouraged, and be passive learners. Self-efficacy is defined as the degree to which a person believes that they will be able to accomplish a certain task and that they are able to exert positive control over events in their lives. Improving self-efficacy may be more complicated than most of the other protective factors due to the hidden nature and inability to observe a person's beliefs. Self-efficacy is the belief that one can achieve what one sets out to do and that one can assert power over the environment to accomplish something.

Nelsen et al. (2000) describe self-efficacy using what they call the three empowering perceptions: "I am capable," "I have the power to make choices that influence what happens to me," and "I contribute in meaningful ways and I am genuinely needed." Self-efficacy is related to the basic psychological needs of power and freedom. Basically, students with poor self-efficacy tend to have an external locus of control. In other words, they believe events outside their control determine success, and they often fail to make the connection between their effort and successful results. They do not feel powerful enough or believe they can influence events. Simply stated, they do not believe they will be successful.

Two effective ways to improve the self-efficacy of students is by providing them with meaningful roles and structuring their academic success. Finding meaningful roles for students—in the classroom, school, or community—is very important in developing self-efficacy and resilience. Examples of meaningful roles within the classroom include running errands, taking attendance, passing out papers, timing and checking work, problem solving, working as the teacher's aide, and peer and cross-age tutoring. I know one teacher who enlisted the help of one of her difficult students who had a great deal of specific knowledge and interest in computers. The teacher gave him the role of classroom expert on computer issues, and the other students were directed to him when they had questions about the computer. Service learning, which has had much attention recently, is an excellent way to build self-efficacy. In community service learning projects, students learn they can contribute in important ways and that they are genuinely needed. Structuring for success might include setting realistically high expectations for the student (these may or may not correlate with course of study or curricular goals), teaching the skills necessary to perform the task, providing much feedback throughout the task, and engaging the student in self-evaluation of his or her performance.

Glenn and Nelsen's (1989) book *Raising Self-Reliant Children in a Self-Indulgent World* provides useful information on self-efficacy for teachers. In addition, self-efficacy is closely related to optimism. They both involve beliefs, attributions, and explanations of events.

OPTIMISM

Students who lack optimism are prone to give up easily when challenged or initially unsuccessful and are also prone to helplessness, dependence, and even depression. Optimists see failure as due to something that they are able to influence, which leads them to believe that the next time they can be successful. Optimism is much more than positive thinking. Optimism is what Seligman (1995) calls nonnegative thinking. Optimistic individuals explain negative events in their lives as temporary, specific, and nonpersonal, whereas pessimists tend to explain negative events by saying, "It's me, it will last forever, and it's going to affect everything else." Optimism is not overly flowery or positive but based on realistic logic.

For example, when Tammy gets a poor grade on her spelling test, she may say to herself, "I just can't get spelling. I hate it!" This self-explanation is pessimistic in that it is personal, long-term or permanent, and pervasive (i.e., generalized from one test to spelling in general). Tammy could be taught to reframe this explanation in a nonnegative fashion, such as, "I did poorly on this test. Maybe I could study more next time." Notice the second thought is not overly positive or flowery, such as "I'm the best speller in the school." It is more realistic, temporary, and specific. If you teach students to be positive thinkers with statements such as "Everything will work out great," they will turn off since often things do not work out great.

Optimism is a skill that can be modeled, encouraged, and taught to students. Figure 5.5 provides examples of optimistic reframing that teachers can use in the classroom. Teaching students to be optimistic involves teaching them to how to recognize and dispute their pessimistic beliefs or explanations of events. Research has shown that parents and teachers who have negative or pessimistic explanatory styles can inadvertently teach students pessimistic ways of explaining events (Seligman, 1995). In short, teachers need to model optimism in front of their students when they experience a negative event or make a mistake.

Optimistic individuals resist depression and unhappiness in large part by how they explain events that happen to them (Seligman, 1995). Optimism is also a key component in resilience. Students who maintain hope, see problems as learning experiences, and who do not take problems personally are able to withstand adversity. Seligman has shown that a person's level of optimism or explanatory style is predictive of success at work, in the family, in sports, in health, and at school. In fact, optimists with the same level of measured potential outperform or exceed their potential, and pessimists drop below their potential (Seligman, 1990). Seligman (1995) concludes, "I have come to think that the notion of potential, without the notion of optimism, has very little meaning" (p. 154). Readers interested in curriculum related to optimism are referred to the Penn Prevention Project (Seligman, 1995) for more information.

Figure 5.5 Optimistic Reframing

Negative Event	Self-Statement	Optimistic Reframe
• Poor report card	I guess I'm just stupid.	I slacked this time; next grading period I can do better.
• Fight with friend	She never listens to me. We will never make up.	Lately she has not been listening to me. We get along better when we are alone and can talk it out.
• Difficulty learning	I'm in the stupid class. I hate school.	I'm doing so well with decimals. I have to work really hard at school and especially at math.
• Being teased or bullied	Everybody always teases me. Maybe they are right: I will never have any friends.	Jason and his friends tease me sometimes. Maybe they do it because they want to fit in and think they are cool. Robert never teases me.

SUMMARY OF MAIN POINTS

• Teachers who model and teach social-emotional skills increase student learning, resilience, and positive relationships and decrease misbehavior.

• There are many strategies and promising and effective programs available to assist teachers in enhancing student social skills, problem solving, self-control, self-efficacy, and optimism.

• Conflict resolution trains students to understand conflict and increases their ability to seek win-win solutions by using the techniques of negotiation, mediation, and consensus decision making.

• Teachers play a key role in intervening and preventing bullying by understanding victims and bullies, teaching students about bullying, establishing consequences for bullying, and encouraging bystanders to report bullying.

• Teachers can model and teach optimism. Optimists explain negative events that happen to them in a temporary, realistic, specific, and nonpersonal fashion. Teachers can help students recognize pessimistic thoughts and explanations and dispute them.

QUESTIONS FOR DISCUSSION AND SELF-EVALUATION

1. What barriers may be in place that would prevent you from implementing social-emotional skill building in your classroom or school?

2. In what ways do you already build these skills in your classroom?

3. Does your behavior in the classroom model effective social-emotional skills?

4. Do the classroom management strategies in your classroom increase the development of social skills, problem solving, self-control, self-efficacy, and optimism?

5. Of the five social-emotional skills discussed, which one is most important for a student to succeed in school and life?

ACTION PLAN

As a result of something that I learned in this chapter I plan to (be specific in your answer):

_____

_____

_____

RECOMMENDED RESOURCES

Bodine, R., Crawford, D., & Schrumpf, F. (1994). *Creating the peaceable school: A comprehensive program for teaching conflict resolution.* Champaign, IL: Research Press. This is an excellent program for learning the skills of conflict resolution. The book focuses on building a peaceful climate and understanding conflict and peace and the three types of conflict resolution. It also includes a companion student manual.

Elias, M., Zins, J., Weissberg, R., Frey, K., Greenberg, M., Haynes, N., et al. (1997). *Promoting social and emotional learning: Guidelines for educators.* Alexandria, VA: Association for Supervision and Curriculum Development. This book delineates promising strategies and practices for teaching social-emotional skills to students.

Kagan, S. (1994). *Cooperative learning.* San Juan Capistrano, CA: Kagan Cooperative Learning. This classic work in cooperative learning also gives many strategies to build social, communication, and thinking skills of students.

Seligman, M. (1995). *The optimistic child.* New York: HarperCollins. This book discusses strategies to teach students to be optimistic and details how parental and teacher explanatory styles influence the style of their children.

CHAPTER SIX

Enhancing Student Motivation

"Nothing is so unequal as the equal treatment of unequals."

—Thomas Jefferson

CHAPTER OBJECTIVES

In this chapter the reader will learn:

- Instructional strategies that increase achievement and decrease misbehavior
- Strategies that increase motivation and decrease misbehavior
- How beliefs on adapting instruction influence teacher behavior
- A framework for adapting instruction using nine types of adaptations

Academic success is also a focus of a relationship-driven classroom. Academic failure is a serious risk factor. It has been estimated that people with histories of school failure commit 82% of all crime, and more than 85% of youth affiliated with the court system are illiterate (Adams, 1990). If our goal in a relationship-driven classroom is to eliminate the underlying causes of misbehavior, we can't overlook academic failure as a contributing cause to the behavior. Therefore, the relationship-driven classroom strives to eliminate failure and promote academic success. Students will go to great lengths to avoid tasks when they do not feel that they can be successful. They would much rather be seen as a rebel, troublemaker, or class clown than be viewed as dumb.

Students may choose effective and ineffective behaviors to meet their needs. For example, if their power or achievement need is frustrated, they are likely to try to meet this need by being good at something else, namely misbehaving. In fact, research shows that misbehavior is sometimes a response to academic failure and that when these students were provided opportunities to experience academic and social success, their behavior improved (Gettinger, 1988).

One important component discussed in Chapter 1 was setting high expectations for student achievement and providing the necessary supports to achieve the expectations (Benard, 1995). We must not forget the second part of this statement—"with the necessary supports." This chapter is about providing the necessary supports by using instructional strategies that increase achievement and motivation and decrease misbehavior and by adapting instruction for diverse learners.

INSTRUCTIONAL STRATEGIES THAT INCREASE ACHIEVEMENT AND REDUCE MISBEHAVIOR

Classroom misbehavior can be prevented when effective instructional strategies are used because students are engaged and are experiencing success. On the other hand, when students are not engaged or they or do not feel successful, misbehavior often occurs. Educational research has revealed numerous effective instructional strategies (Marzano, Pickering, & Pollock, 2001). In this section I focus on maintaining active student involvement, setting clear and personalized learning objectives, and providing effective feedback and recognition.

Maintaining Active Student Involvement

Academic engaged time, or the amount of time students are actually engaged in learning tasks, is critical to achievement and behavior management. The more students are engaged and involved in a lesson, the less misbehavior they will display (Evertson & Harris, 2003). Active involvement or engagement can be maximized by increasing student opportunities to respond, ensuring high rates of success, and varying learning formats.

Increasing Student Opportunities to Respond

Teacher talk is speaking or lecturing for an extended time without involving students. Teachers should take into consideration the amount of communication that is teacher produced versus student produced. Generally, teachers should only talk for a few minutes before involving students by asking questions or giving a task. One way to increase student involvement is to use the instruct-write process. In this strategy the teacher pauses at a natural stopping point in the lecture and asks the students to write down the key points and any questions from the lecture. The teacher can continue instructing and repeat the process. After the instruct-write process has occurred a few times, student pairs can discuss the key ideas they derived from the lecture and any questions they have. The teacher is able to then summarize the most important points and answer common questions.

One of the best ways to increase student opportunities to respond and to check for understanding at the same time is to ask a question and then allow all students to write their answer either on a sheet of paper or a slate board. Slate boards are unique because they allow the teacher to easily scan student answers. This tactic has an obvious advantage over asking one student for an oral response: It requires all students to participate, rather than just one. The key to remember is that when students are talking or writing about instructional information, they tend to be more involved and engaged than when they are just listening.

Ensuring High Rates of Success

Students are more apt to stay involved in tasks when they are reaching success. Teachers can help ensure high rates of academic success by checking for understanding during both lessons and practice. All students need to respond during a lesson, either in unison or individually. One efficient way to monitor understanding is to check the understanding of low-functioning students. If low-functioning students are progressing, it is likely that the majority of students understand. Effective teachers provide enough instruction and modeling to ensure that students can perform most tasks at 90% accuracy. On more difficult tasks effective teachers allow for more teacher-directed practice and modeling before independent work (Sprick et al., 1998). Another useful strategy is to provide students with an answer key, so they can periodically check their independent work. Too often we only check for understanding by asking if there are any questions, in which case we may really be checking for bravery since students risk looking foolish if they ask questions. A better way to check for understanding would be to have a colored card at the top or side of each student's desk. A flipped-over card indicates to the teacher that the student needs assistance. Another strategy is to just mention some possible questions that students might have and ask the class to answer them.

Using a Variety of Learning Formats

Effective teachers use a variety of learning formats, or ways to orchestrate student learning, in their classroom to maintain active student involvement. Research has shown that students prefer a variety of learning formats (Evertson & Harris, 2003). Some common learning formats are whole-group lecture, teacher-directed small-group, cooperative group, student pairs, and individual formats. These groups are formed by the teacher and are based on the needs of students and the information to be learned. For example, a teacher-directed small group is usually desired for a group with specific and common needs. A cooperative group format is preferred when the purpose is to practice learned information or to create a product based on learned content, and is usually made up of a variety of students. Cooperative groups have been shown to increase student involvement and participation. This is especially true when students are taught effective small-group behavior and both group and individual grades are used (Evertson & Harris, 2003). One caution for teachers when using varied learning formats is to be aware that students often will need to be taught the expectations and procedures for each format. The reader is directed to Evertson and Harris (2003) for an excellent description of different learning formats.

In summary, using strategies that increase student opportunities to respond, ensuring high rates of student success, and incorporating varied learning formats can increase student involvement and academic engagement time. Another strategy that enhances student learning and decreases misbehavior is setting learning objectives for students.

Setting Clear and Personalized Learning Objectives

Learning is enhanced when teachers set goals or objectives for learning that are made explicit to the students. Effective teachers start each unit or lesson by communicating or writing the expected learning goals, which then drives student and teacher behavior toward internalizing the goals. However, these objectives should not be so specific or rigid that students are unable to personalize them to meet their needs and interests. When students set subgoals based on the general learning objectives set by the teacher, it can have a powerful effect on learning (Marzano et al., 2001).

Teachers can assist students in setting personalized learning goals by first discussing the general class objectives. From there, students are asked what specific knowledge they are curious about or interested in gaining from the topic. For example, an elementary student had heard that daddy longlegs were not really spiders. He decided that his personalized goal in a unit on insects would be to discover if this was true and, if so, why they were not classified as spiders. Students could formalize these personalized goals by discussing them with the teacher and writing them down. Some teachers use goal notebooks for personalized academic or behavior goals, in which the teacher confers with the student and assists in the development and the monitoring of progress toward the student's goals. Some teachers build on this process by allowing students to contract for a specific grade if they meet their goals.

Providing Effective Feedback

Effective teachers use both supportive and corrective feedback in their classrooms. Feedback is an important component for both academics and behavior. One critical aspect of feedback is time or immediacy. Generally speaking, the longer one has to wait for feedback after performing a task, the less effective the feedback is. Immediacy of feedback is especially important when students are practicing a new skill, so the teachers can ensure that the students are not practicing the wrong process or making frequent errors. One way to prevent students from practicing errors is to check the first response of all students during independent practice settings.

Effective feedback is immediate, frequent, and specific. For example, students should receive their tests back in a timely fashion, with explanations of accurate and inaccurate responses, and with feedback about areas of specific knowledge or skill. Research also suggests that achievement is increased when students are asked to continue working on test items until they succeed (Marzano et al., 2001). When students give an incorrect oral or written response, it is important to acknowledge if some part of the answer is accurate and to support and guide the student to the correct answer. Similarly, it is important to recognize when students get part of the process right but not the end product. Both process and end product are important.

Giving Rewards and Recognition

Rewards and recognition have come under attack with claims that they hinder intrinsic motivation. In fact, rewards, when used effectively, increase achievement and intrinsic motivation (Marzano et al., 2001). Effective teachers realize that students need positive recognition, and some students require more than others. However, in situations where students display appropriate behavior or do exactly as the teacher directs, they receive reward or praise only 15% of the time. In addition, negative reprimands are evident every 2 to 5 minutes in the average classroom (Algozzine & Ysseldyke, 1997). We need to be vigilant in acknowledging positive behavior more than negative behavior and using effective reward and recognition practices.

Rewards, like feedback, are most effective when they are immediate, frequent, and specific. It is important that rewards not be too easily earned or too difficult to earn. Praising students for accomplishing easy tasks can have a negative impact on achievement and motivation. Rewards are most effective when given in response for students accomplishing specific goals as opposed to rewarding them for completion of the work regardless of quality or standard (Algozzine & Ysseldyke, 1997). Rewards that are given solely for task completion do hinder intrinsic motivation. In addition, verbal reward or social praise seems to be more effective than tangible (i.e., candy, money, food, stickers) rewards. If tangible rewards are used, they should be used for accomplishing a specific standard of performance and faded out for more social rewards.

Some examples of social rewards are a handshake, time with a preferred friend or teacher, a special job, public recognition, a positive phone call home, or a written note from teacher to student. One caution to remember is that rewards are valued differently by everyone. In other words, not all students will find the same things rewarding. While eating lunch with the teacher may be rewarding for some, it may be punishment for others. There are numerous ways to use rewards or recognition in the classroom. Two unique and effective strategies for using rewards are lotteries and unpredictable celebrations.

Lotteries

A lottery strategy (Algozzine & Ysseldyke, 1997) can be implemented with a roll of raffle tickets and a box. In this positive approach students write short answers to teacher questions on the back of the lottery tickets. For example, students could write the main idea of a story, answer a riddle, answer a math problem, or even list a positive behavior that the teacher noticed on the back of the ticket. Students then put their name and date on the tickets and place them in the lottery box. The teacher then sets a classwide criterion that must be met to earn a lottery drawing. For example, the criterion could be that each time students complete a successful and timely transition, the teacher will give the students a tally mark. Once 10 tally marks are earned, a lottery drawing takes place. Students are motivated to earn as many tickets as they can to increase their chances of winning. In addition, the whole class is motivated to earn a lottery drawing.

Unpredictable Celebrations

Unpredictable celebrations can be a powerful form of reward and recognition. This strategy involves giving recognition or reward to a student or class for some important accomplishment.

It is unpredictable in the sense that celebrations are not given for every occurrence of the behavior, and students are not aware beforehand what the reward will be. According to Sprick et al. (1998), "The key is to use these celebrations as sparingly as possible, but as frequently as necessary (and always unpredictably!) to keep students proud and excited about their achievements" (p. 221). Younger students may enjoy celebrations involving extra recess time, eating lunch with the teacher, or a special activity. Older students may enjoy extra free time for the entire class, time with a favorite peer, or a free homework pass.

In summary, effective teachers enhance academic success and indirectly reduce misbehavior by increasing student active involvement, by setting clear and personal learning goals, and by providing frequent feedback and recognition. In the next section I address strategies that improve motivation. The reader will notice some overlap and commonalities between instructional strategies that increase academic success and the strategies that increase motivation.

INSTRUCTIONAL STRATEGIES THAT INCREASE MOTIVATION AND REDUCE MISBEHAVIOR

Teachers can have much influence on reducing misbehavior by using strategies that increase student motivation to learn. Although sometimes it may seem that teachers have little control over student motivation, research has shown that teachers can influence student motivation at all ages (Anderman & Midgley, 1998). Generally speaking, this research indicates that students need work that enhances their sense of competency; allows them to develop relationships with others; gives them a degree of freedom, choice, and autonomy; and provides opportunities for originality and self-expression. In the following sections, I take a closer look at how positive relationships, providing student choice, attribution theory, and increasing task value and expectancy can build student motivation.

Positive Relationships

When thinking about student motivation, it is tempting to look solely at the student, but we must also look at the learning environment. What is present in classrooms when student motivation is high? A necessary precondition for any motivational strategy is creating a positive classroom climate. If students experience care, respect, support, trust, and a sense of belonging in the classroom, they will participate more fully in the process of learning; on the other hand, if students feel alienated or isolated, their energies are directed toward self-protection and acceptance, not learning.

Motivation to learn is enhanced when there is a strong and personal relationship between teacher and student (Mendler, 2000). When students perceive that the teacher likes them and that the teacher cares about their needs, their level of involvement and motivation increases. Would you rather do quality work for a boss who is controlling, unfriendly, threatening, critical, and assuming or one who is friendly, warm, supportive, empowering, and encouraging? Fear of punishment does not usually result in quality work.

Student Choice

When we give choices to students about their learning, self-determination, shared ownership, involvement, and motivation all are enhanced. We could foster motivation by allowing student choice on issues such as room decoration, whether they want to work in a group or independently, the type of assignment or project, choice of books for a book report, seating and room arrangements, type of celebration, and field trips. One useful strategy is to ask the students after introducing the topic, "What do you think would be the most interesting way we could learn about this topic?" Allowing students to choose personal learning goals based on lesson objectives, as mentioned in the previous section, increases motivation as well.

Attribution Theory

Another important motivation concept is attribution. Attribution theory can be easily conceptualized using a hierarchy of desirable attributions. Generally speaking, we want students to attribute their successes and failures first to effort. It is less desirable for our students to attribute success and failure to luck or someone or something else (i.e., "The test was easy"). Attribution theory suggests that motivation and persistence are enhanced when students attribute their success and failure to causes that they are able to control (e.g., insufficient effort and preparation) as opposed to being outside their control (e.g., ability or bad luck). Teachers can assist students in developing more effective attributions by encouraging students to view failures as temporary and changeable and due to factors such as lack of information, poor strategy choices, or lack of preparation. Teachers can model these types of attributions by acknowledging and discussing teacher mistakes and attributing them to temporary and controllable factors. In addition, when teachers use effective praise, it may help students attribute their successes to effort and preparation. When we attribute success to ability only, we can actually undermine future achievement and motivation (Evertson & Harris, 2003).

Increasing Task Value and Expectancy

Motivation, like behavior, can be a quite complex subject. Each individual has his or her own motivation system. A useful way for teachers to conceptualize student motivation is that the effort that students are willing to put forth on a task is related to both the degree to which they expect to be successful and the degree to which they value the rewards that it will bring (Brophy & Good, 2000). In other words, both expectancy and task value are critical in predicting student motivation. Therefore, if teachers wish to maximize motivation, they should strive to help students understand the value of school activities and structure tasks so that student effort leads to success.

We can increase task value by first helping students make a connection between what they will be learning and how and why it is important to them. One teacher helped her geometry students make this connection by allowing them to work with the city director to design a parking lot that would maximize parking. A reading teacher can enhance task value by showing students what types of books or words they will be able to read if they are willing to put forth the effort. A middle school science teacher increased task value by showing students a model submarine and telling them they would be designing their own submarine after learning the concepts of buoyancy and density. Keep in mind that students tend to think in the near present. Statements such as

"You will need to know this for next year" or "If you become an engineer" or "If you want to do well on the test" do not usually build task value.

In addition to these strategies for increasing motivation, the following additional strategies are adapted from Brophy and Good (2000) for building student motivation:

- *Ask questions of personal value and importance rather than just fact during discussions.* Instead of asking, "What year did Columbus discover the new world?" one could ask questions about why the trip did not take place sooner or if students would have volunteered if asked to go. Ask opinion as well as fact questions.

- *Induce curiosity by using mystery, novelty, fantasy, suspense, controversy and conflict, contradictions, and inductive reasoning.* By using activities that create discrepancies between their beliefs and expectations, students have an inner need to reduce the inconsistency. By eliciting conflict and differing opinions about a topic, students are motivated to prove their viewpoint. This technique has the added benefit of teaching conflict resolution. Use the joy of discovery by giving students information and asking them to develop hypotheses and conclusions.

- *Build on internal motivation.* Students are motivated by both internal and external rewards (intrinsic and extrinsic motivation). However, it is important to keep in mind that the motivation level and quality of work is higher when students are working for self-interest rather than to escape punishment, to please an adult, or to obtain a reward. Intrinsic motivation is maximized when tasks are adequately but not too challenging, novel and interesting, and make-believe and when students have real choices in what and how they learn.

- *Do not emphasize grades or comparisons, just quality work and progress.* Focus on mastery, personal success, and improvement rather than comparing a student's performance to others'. All children will not have the same criteria for success. Allow for self-evaluation or use rubrics to let students have a role in their own assessment. Students are more willing to take learning risks and ask questions when personal success is honored more so than relative success to others.

- *Alter the audience.* Have students share learning products with people outside the classroom. Parents, community members, politicians, principals, and support staff are good audiences.

The teacher in a relationship-driven classroom routinely self-evaluates the effectiveness of instruction in terms of enhancing achievement and motivation and reducing misbehavior. In addition, the relationship-driven teacher understands the importance of adapting instruction to meet individual student needs.

ADAPTING INSTRUCTION
FOR DIVERSE LEARNERS

Adapting instruction becomes critical as classes become more diverse and inclusive of students with disabilities. It is not uncommon for a teacher to have students with IQs of 140 in the same class with students who have IQs below 70. Research has revealed that the average range of instructional levels in a regular education class is five grade levels (Jenkins, Pious, & Jewell, 1990). In addition, the students that we are asked to educate have more emotional and behavioral problems that interfere with learning (Doll, 1994).

Relationship-driven teachers honor diversity and model tolerance. They do so not only in religion, race, creed, and color but also in cognitive or academic diversity. They use instructional strategies and adaptations to maximize the success of diverse learners, and they have a deep understanding of the interrelationship between academic success and behavior.

To understand adaptive instruction I examine common beliefs and misconceptions about adapting instruction and the nine types of adaptations. The Resource at the end of this book contains lists of general instructional practices that accommodate diverse learners as well as some specific adaptations in the areas of note taking, organization, presentation of directions, homework, tests, and grades.

Beliefs About Adapting Instruction

I have found that about a third of teachers want to adapt instruction and say, "Just show me how." Another third naturally adapt instruction by using a variety of instructional practices within their classrooms, and a final third do not believe in the practice. The section on beliefs is really for this final third group.

Beliefs influence behavior. As I have consulted with teachers over the years, I have found a number of deeply held beliefs about adapting instruction. These beliefs are not good or bad. However, they do influence whether or not, and to what degree, teachers will modify, adapt, or adjust their instructional practices to meet diverse learning needs. The following two lists are by no means exhaustive. I have found that teachers will not be able to successfully adapt instruction without coming to terms with some of these underlying beliefs. I advocate that we examine our beliefs and ask, "Does it help to look at things this way?" In the next section, I examine some of these beliefs in more detail.

Beliefs That Facilitate Adaptive Instruction

- Academic goals need not be the same for each learner.

- Adaptation is desirable for any student who is not experiencing success in the classroom.

- Adaptation is essential for students working above grade level as well as for those working below grade level.

- Adaptations help to accommodate the wide range of student abilities in the typical classroom.

- Adaptations demonstrate acceptance and respect of individual learning differences.

Beliefs That Impede Adaptive Instruction

- All students in the same class should be similar in ability levels.

- Students with special or diverse needs are better off in a special education room.

- I do not have the expertise to work with special needs students.

- There is not enough time to make the necessary adaptations.

- Adaptations will create lowered expectations.

- It is not fair to adapt for individual students.

- My job is to teach the course of study objectives.

The Rationale for Adaptive Instruction

In this section I examine five of the most common arguments against adapting instruction. I have named these arguments priority of course of study, fairness, laziness, lowered expectations, sanctity of the grading system, and preparation for next year.

Priority of Course of Study

Recently, I was conducting staff development for some teachers in a nearby county. The topic was adapting instruction for student success, a timely topic given the move toward inclusion. As I was discussing developing alternate goals for students who have deficient skills or who are not experiencing success, a young teacher raised her hand and said, "But I get paid to teach the course of study." She went on to describe that if the course of study lists fractions, then she teaches fractions. I responded by validating the importance of the course of study to a certain degree. A problem exists when the course of study is given more authority than the teacher's professional opinion about what is best for an individual student. Is our job to teach the student or teach the course of study? What if fractions are an inappropriate goal for some students in the class? Should a student who is two or more years below grade level in reading be given alternative reading materials at his or her instruction level?

My point is that teachers are professionals who may need to adapt the curriculum or course of study to a particular learner's special needs. A course of study should be used as a guideline not a rulebook for instruction. For example, you may teach the whole class to add fractions, but for a few students the goal may not be mastery of adding fractions; it might be mastery of identifying numerator and denominator or mastery in comparing fractions. Principals can facilitate this individualized approach to the curriculum not only by giving teachers permission to adapt as necessary but also by letting them know that adaptation is expected.

Fairness

Some teachers feel that adapting instruction is unfair, unless students are in special education. Is it fair to assume that all students are at the same level and should have the same goals? Ironically, this so-called fairness is the greatest inequity of all. That we should expect the same from all students is like a doctor or nurse expecting the patients to be the same and have the same medical needs. A similar analogy would be if you had insulin for a diabetic student but withheld it because it would not fair to rest of the students. When we do not provide individualized support for students under the guise of fairness, it is like withholding insulin from a diabetic student because there is not enough insulin for every student. Adapting instruction is important for any student who is not experiencing success in the classroom, not just students with disabilities. This could include gifted, emotionally troubled, and disabled students; students under temporary stress; or even immature students. Our students come to us with such tremendous developmental diversity. We then somewhat arbitrarily say, "This is what someone your age should know." Anyone who has even been around middle school students can attest to the developmental diversity that exists during these years. Some students look like young adults, while some look like young children. Do we accept and honor this physical diversity more so than cognitive diversity?

Laziness

The next argument that I frequently encounter is that students are lazy. The teachers state, "Why should we adapt instruction if the student is just not doing the work?" This is a legitimate question on the surface. However, my response typically is "Because it is not working." For example, I sometimes recommend shortening homework assignments for students who have not been completing assignments. I make this recommendation whether or not the student has a disability. Wouldn't it be better to get some of something than all of nothing?

The point is not that there are no lazy students but that there are often more complex reasons why the student is not choosing to or is unable to produce. What skill or skills is the student lacking? Is it possible that the student wants you and the other students to think that he or she doesn't care? Why is the student unwilling to take a risk? Are there any other classes where this student is being productive and successful? When was the last time this student was successful in the classroom? What was different then? Does the student have any hope or any self-efficacy belief that he or she can accomplish the tasks? When we label a student as lazy, we are placing all the responsibility for the problem and its solution on the student.

Lowered Expectations

The third argument I receive about adaptive instruction is that it may water down the curriculum or lower expectations that we set for our students. Research on effective teachers and schools reveals that adapting instruction is one characteristic of effectiveness (Algozzine & Ysseldyke, 1997). There is no evidence that students from classrooms that use adaptive instruction score lower on achievement tests (Deschenes, Ebeling, & Sprague, 1994). Adapting instruction does not dumb down instruction but makes it receivable for all or most learners. The goal of adaptation is to make typical lessons more accessible or receivable to more students. For example, we know that only a small minority of the population prefers auditory information in learning, yet the majority of the instruction is presented verbally. Are we lowering our standards if we attempt to decrease the amount of auditory information in the classroom? Or are we making information more receivable to our students?

Sanctity of the Grading System

The next argument that I typically receive about adaptive instruction is that it will hurt the grading system. Teachers argue that if one student receives adaptations during the grading period and ends up with a grade of C, and another student receives no adaptations and also ends up with a C, the grading system is tarnished. The argument is that a C, or any grade for that matter, for one student should equal a C for all students. Their concerns are that it is unfair to other students and that a future teacher may see that grade and be misled by it.

My question is, "If two students earn a C and one student did little studying while the other studied 3 hours, should both earn a C?" Interestingly, many teachers feel that the student who worked harder should get the higher grade. So a C may not equal a C in this case. As far as misleading future teachers, I'm not sure how many teachers go through student records to determine what letter grade a particular student received in a prior subject.

Grades are not as objective and fair as many believe. For example, on a pretest one student receives 100% and another receives 25%. On the spelling test the student who received 25% improved by spelling five more words correctly. Her final grade for this test was 50%. Is it objective or fair that a student who gains five words gets a failing grade and a student who makes no gains receives an A? Grades may reward mastery but punish growth. In addition, grades may predict which students were better able to decipher what the teacher wants (Curwin & Mendler, 1999a). The sanctity of grades is further diminished because grades often do not predict future success (Goleman, 1995). Perhaps grading should be more narrative and flexible instead of simply a letter, which would allow for effort, attitude, and improvement. This brings me to the final argument on adaptations.

Preparation for Next Year

Teachers resist adaptations under the notion that they are not preparing the student for the next year. As the receiving teacher, I would rather have a student who gained some skills rather than a student who made no progress at all. Instead of focusing on preparing for next year, why not take that student from where he or she is and make progress from there? Effectiveness is best defined by student growth from a starting point (Tomlinson, 1999).

By focusing on the future and rigidly holding to the arbitrary grade-level curriculum or course of study, we may be reducing the chance for student success and further alienating students from school. We may pay a premium price for refusing to adapt instruction. The price may be student failure, dropout, alienation, poor motivation, and poor behavior. One of the key protective factors of resiliency is experiencing a caring and supportive environment. Students in classrooms where adaptive instruction and grading are commonplace rate it as more caring and supportive whether or not they are the recipients of the adaptations (Deschenes et al., 1994). The following nine types of adaptations provide a framework for conceptualizing adaptive instruction for both low-performing and advanced students.

Nine Types of Adaptations

This framework, created by Deschenes et al. (1994), is meant to be a framework from which other adaptations can be created. The nine adaptations include size, time, level of support, input, difficulty, output, participation, alternate goals, and substitute curriculum. What follows is a brief description of each adaptation and some examples:

1. *Size.* The number of items the student is expected to complete or learn is reduced or increased. For example, a student struggling with math may be asked to complete a fewer number of problems. A student who is struggling in spelling may be given a smaller list. A student excelling in social studies might be asked to learn more characteristics of the executive branch of government.

2. *Time.* The allotted time for learning, testing, or task completion is altered. For example, the pace of instruction can be varied for some students. A student who is struggling in a subject may be given extra time to practice or master a concept before a test. A student who has a difficult time writing may require more time to complete the test.

3. *Level of support.* The amount of individualized attention to the student is increased or decreased. For example, the teacher could assign a room volunteer or peer tutor to work on spelling words with a student.

4. *Input.* The manner in which instruction is delivered to the students is adapted. For example, on a difficult lesson a teacher could plan to use more concrete examples. The teacher could allow students to teach a lesson or perform a role-play or skit. A poor reader could use books on tape, and advanced students might benefit from using more abstract examples, such as metaphors or analogies.

5. *Difficulty.* The skill or instructional level is reduced or enhanced. The rules of task completion can also be adapted. For example, students who struggle with multiplication may use a calculator for solving word problems.

6. *Output.* The student may use different ways to respond or display mastery. For example, a student with a fine motor weakness could respond with an oral response instead of a motor, or written, one. Instead of an essay test, some students could dictate their answers to a peer or tape recorder. A student may complete a project rather than take a test to reveal what he or she knows.

7. *Participation.* The extent that the student is involved in the lesson is altered. For example, in science lab a student may be required to keep track of time on a stopwatch or given the role of encourager in a cooperative group. A student may participate by holding the globe, while the other students practice geography.

8. *Alternate goals.* The goals or objectives are adapted within the same lesson and materials. For example, a student may not be held accountable for spelling the states correctly or may need to identify the numerator and denominator of a fraction rather than the operation. An advanced student could be required to know not only the primary but also the secondary causes of the Civil War.

9. *Substitute curriculum.* Students receive different instruction and materials to reach a goal. For example, during math a low-functioning student could work on money skills. In reading, an advanced student could read a more advanced novel.

This framework is useful because teachers can use this model to develop many different adaptations for severely disabled students, struggling students, and advanced students. Keep in mind that the goal is not to develop a whole new curriculum or lesson for individual students but to make typical lessons more accessible to all students. More information on specific adaptations for students who are having difficulty in the areas of note taking, organization, interpretation of directions, homework, tests, and grades is located in the Resource Section.

SUMMARY OF MAIN POINTS

- Student behavior cannot be separated from academic success and failure.

- Effective teachers use strategies that increase academic success and motivation and reduce misbehavior.

- Teachers must examine their beliefs and practices related to low-achieving students and making adaptations.

- To meet the increasing diversity of needs of our students we must adapt the curriculum, the instruction, or both.

- The nine types of adaptations are a useful starting point for teachers to begin adapting instruction.

- A protective factor of resilience is experiencing a supportive and caring environment. When we honor all types of diversity, including academic and cognitive diversity, we are creating a supporting and caring environment.

QUESTIONS FOR
DISCUSSION AND SELF-EVALUATION

1. Do you see a connection between academic success and behavior in your classroom?

2. What are some benefits to the classroom teacher in allowing student choices in learning?

3. What techniques or strategies do you use to increase motivation?

4. What are some ways teachers could increase the number of acknowledgments of positive behavior and decrease the number of negative comments about behavior?

5. What are some beliefs about adapting instruction that you may have or that you may have heard that help or hinder meeting diverse learners' success?

ACTION PLAN

As a result of something that I learned in this chapter I plan to (be specific in your answer):

_____

_____

_____

RECOMMENDED RESOURCES

Algozzine, B., & Ysseldyke, J. (1997). *Strategies and tactics for effective instruction.* Longmont, CO: Sopris West. The purpose of this book is to provide teachers with specific and research-proven tactics to plan, manage, deliver, and evaluate classroom instruction.

Deschenes, C., Ebeling, D., & Sprague, J. (1994). *Adapting curriculum and instruction in inclusive classrooms: A teacher's desk reference.* Bloomington, IN: Institute for the Study of

Developmental Disabilities. This book explains seven steps for adapting curriculum and instruction and the nine types of adaptations used for diverse learners.

Glasser, W. (2000). *Every student can succeed.* San Diego, CA: Black Forest Press. This book looks at some new ideas for enhancing the success for all learners, including applying choice theory to the classroom and a new concept called total learning competency.

Marzano, R., Pickering, D., & Pollock, J. (2001). *Classroom instruction that works: Research-based strategies for increasing student achievement.* Alexandria, VA: Association for Supervision and Curriculum Development. This book focuses on nine instructional strategies that have been shown to increase academic achievement across many educational research studies. The book explains educational research in simple terms and focuses on effect size and percentile gain.

CHAPTER SEVEN

Enhancing Student Responsibility

"If you want true power, you must give some of it away."

—Author Unknown

CHAPTER OBJECTIVES

In this chapter the reader will learn:

- The difference between responsibility and obedience
- The side effects of punishment
- How choices increase student responsibility
- How to incorporate self-management strategies
- The WDEP system of conversation
- Action planning and goal setting

Relationship-driven classrooms put more emphasis on teaching responsibility than on punishing misbehavior. In this chapter I discuss some myths surrounding responsibility and the difference between responsibility and obedience. In addition, I investigate strategies to enhance student responsibility, such as using choices effectively, using self-management strategies, and using the WDEP system of conversation.

It is vital to understand that teachers can facilitate or impede the development of student responsibility. I described in earlier chapters the importance of teacher consistency, teaching and practicing expectations and procedures, building social-emotional skills, providing clear lesson objectives, and providing feedback and recognition. Ethically, we can't hold a student responsible for behaviors that they are not able to exhibit or for behaviors demonstrated under conditions where the expectations were unclear or assumed. Students will not be able to exhibit responsible behavior, and we will not be able to ethically hold them accountable for responsible behavior, if we do not provide conditions that lead to student responsibility. However, these conditions do not guarantee student responsibility but facilitate its development. In sum, there are critical teacher responsibilities that must be in place if we are going to develop student responsibility.

DEFINING RESPONSIBILITY

Responsibility is a buzzword in education that usually is not specifically defined. Our students may not know what exactly responsibility entails. I recently saw a list of rules at a high school, one of which included the rule "Be Responsible." We need to do more than just tell students to be responsible; simply stating "Be responsible" is too vague for many of our students. What do we want from students specifically in terms of responsibility?

- Responsible people act in a dependable way.

- Responsible people are prompt, prepared, and productive.

- Responsible people avoid making excuses or blaming others for their behaviors.

- Responsible people are able to make effective decisions, even in the absence of an authority figure.

Responsibility is not a skill but a set of many subskills. The building blocks of responsibility are self-awareness, acceptance or ownership of one's behavior, self-evaluation of the effectiveness of one's behavior, planning more effective behaviors, and self-control. Some barriers to responsible behavior include lacking some of the building blocks of responsibility or possibly lacking the skill to exhibit the expected behavior under the right conditions. This chapter is about strategies that teach and foster these building blocks of responsibility.

THE RESPONSIBILITY MYTH

A dangerous assumption is that students should know how to act responsibly and that they purposefully choose not to. When we hold this belief, we may resist providing assistance, prompts, and skill training because we assume that the student should already have the skills. For example, sometimes we make the statement about the student, "That student needs to be more responsible," or we refuse to attempt an intervention, stating, "The student has to be responsible for that." This reasoning is an example of assumptions we make about behavioral skills that we would not make for academics. For example, if a student did not spell a word correctly in a paper, the assumption would most likely be that the student does not know how to spell that word and needs more modeling and practice. What might our first assumption be if a student loses work, has difficulty following directions, or breaks classroom rules? Would our first assumption be that they need to be taught the skills or that they need to have a consequence? The teacher should first determine whether the student understands the expectations and whether or not the student can reasonably accomplish such expectations.

Another aspect of responsibility is giving students opportunities to display responsible behavior through special jobs. Responsibility breeds responsibility (Brendtro, Brokenleg, & VanBockern, 1998). When students are not given responsibilities or ample opportunities to show responsibility, they may be learning irresponsibility. We may unintentionally be sending the message to the student that because they have not acted in a responsible manner in the past they are not able to act responsibly. Many roles exist for students in the classroom, including helping with erasing the boards, running errands, taking attendance, passing out papers, collecting papers, grading papers, and tutoring peers and younger students. Students can even be given opportunities for decision making and planning of classroom practices. There are hundreds more, limited only by one's imagination. These types of responsibilities are largely untapped as a means of preventing discipline problems or as a strategy to connect students to the classroom. In addition, these strategies develop resilience and self-efficacy beliefs that "I am capable and needed and can contribute in a positive way."

One obstacle to using this strategy is the belief that one must earn the privilege to have the responsibility. The students who could benefit the most from this type of meaningful activity are excluded from the opportunity. I recently experienced this belief firsthand. Ginny was a student of high behavioral and academic risk. In a meeting to develop interventions the issue of responsibility arose. One of the teachers stated that the student responded favorably when the teacher gave her classroom responsibilities or chores. The teacher stated that when the student started to "goof off," a reminder was given to her that she could not continue to be a helper if she did not change her behavior. The teacher stated that this strategy was working just fine. I suggested that all the teachers try such an intervention. The other well-meaning teachers stated that they felt uncomfortable providing Ginny with responsibilities because they felt that it would be unfair to the students who were consistently following the rules and that it would be rewarding inappropriate behavior. They felt the other students would resent that Ginny was allowed these privileges.

There are three reasons why I disagree with their belief. First, it is highly unlikely that well-behaving and successful students would resort to negative behaviors to obtain these classroom chores, especially if chores and helping responsibilities are spread out among the students. Second, it presupposes that the other students do not want to see the targeted student succeed and are not aware of his or her special needs. Third, it shows a somewhat distorted understanding of fairness and individual needs. A medical analogy might help prove this point: If a doctor gave the same medicine to all patients, he or she would not be allowed to practice; doctors must diagnose and provide appropriate treatment based on the needs of the patient. In this example, Ginny has different educational needs than many of the other students. Her prescription needs to be different. In the end, Ginny benefited from a structured plan where she was given classroom helper tasks in each class and guidelines for how she must conduct herself to keep these special responsibilities.

Students need plentiful opportunities to display responsible behavior. Are we taking advantage of opportunities to build responsibility in our students? Are special helping roles given equally to all students or just certain types of students?

RESPONSIBILITY VERSUS OBEDIENCE

There is a big difference between obedience and responsibility. Obedience requires the presence of an adult or external control, whereas responsibility requires effective choices with or without the external presence of an adult (Curwin & Mendler, 1999a). Obedience requires compliance with an adult standard or expectation, whereas responsibility requires cooperation, self-control, critical thinking, and decision making. The message of responsibility is that the students are in control of their own choices. Should our goal be student obedience or student responsibility? The difference between external control and self-control provides the real basis for responsibility. Responsible students display self-control rather than having to be policed. The difference between students who are obedient and responsible is manifested when there is a substitute teacher. A certain amount of testing of the limits is normal when a substitute takes over. However, if the behavior is extremely atypical, it may signal that students have operated on a compliance or obedience level that is dependent on you being there versus operating on a responsible level.

The message in obedience is that only adults know what is best for students and students are unable to make effective decisions on their own. Bodine and Crawford (1999) concur by stating that our society is not designed with authorities always directing an individual's actions. McCaslin and Good (1998) delineate three reasons why responsibility and self-management, rather than obedience and compliance, should be stressed:

1. Compliance requires constant monitoring.

2. Compliance that is not internalized does not transfer from one setting to another.

3. Some complex forms of instruction (small-group or cooperative learning) cannot occur if students are dependent or functioning at a sheer compliance level.

PUNISHMENT

Punishment is defined as causing pain, hurt, or loss. The concept that children must experience these feelings to change their behavior is not grounded in fact. This premise has been around for ages and is culturally entrenched, evidenced by the mindset of "get tough on crime." Interestingly, we have been getting tough on crime for some time, and crime has not been deterred (DiGiulio, 2000).

While no one can deny that punishment works in the short term, its long-term effectiveness has been questioned (Brophy & Good, 2000). Punishment does not teach alternative behaviors, self-control, and responsibility; in the short term, it teaches only obedience. Compelling evidence exists that nonpunitive strategies are equally or more effective than punishment in dealing with behavior (LaVigna & Donellan, 1986), and there are more behavior problems in classrooms where the main form of discipline is punishment (Evertson & Harris, 2003).

Side Effects of Punishment

Punishment has numerous side effects that do not enhance the protective factors we are trying to build for our students. Besides its failure to show long-term effectiveness in behavior management, punishment does not and never has enhanced the relationship or bond between teacher and student. Consider these other side effects or drawbacks of traditional punishment:

- Punishment does not teach any replacement behavior; that is, the student is not taught a more effective behavior.

- Punishment often leads to anger, resentment, defensiveness, and retaliation or revenge seeking.

- Punishment does not seek to solve the underlying conflict.

- Punishment often drives the behavior underground. In other words, it is suppressed but not eliminated. When the behavior recovers, punishment must become more intense.

- Punishment increases threat, which inhibits the person's ability to problem solve or do higher level critical thinking.

- Punishment frustrates all the basic psychological needs of belonging, power, freedom, and fun.

- Punishment is focused on past behavior rather than present and future behavior.

- Punishment sends the message that adults solve their problems by force, coercion, or power.

Relationship-driven teachers take into consideration the drawbacks and do not rely on punishment as a classroom management strategy. In addition, they are aware of how punishment can sabotage student responsibility.

How Punishment Hinders Responsibility

Some people believe that the only way students will learn to be responsible is for them to be punished. However, punishment often reduces the development of student responsibility. In fact, some students may actually prefer punishment because they can continue to blame the punisher for their problems instead of taking responsibility themselves. When students are punished, they typically focus their energy on the punishment and the punisher rather than their own behavior. In addition, their energy goes toward coping with the negative feelings that often stem from punishment (embarrassment, disappointment, guilt, anger, resentment, etc.). Remember, responsibility involves awareness, ownership, evaluation, and planning of behavior. When students focus their energy on the punishment and negative emotions, they are not able to accept, evaluate, and plan more effective behavior for the future. If punishment must be used, then it is best when accompanied by teaching and planning more effective behaviors for the future.

CHOICES AND RESPONSIBILITY

Part of being responsible is choosing the right or most effective behavior, which increases the student's level of self-determination. Students who are prevented from choice making in their youth are most likely going to be poor decision makers as adults. We must let our students practice making choices and learn from their mistakes if we want them to get better at decision making and learn to be responsible. To enhance responsibility in our students, we must give and allow choices and encourage self-evaluation of the effectiveness of these choices. Building responsibility through giving choices may be more difficult in the short run but more effective in the long term. It is certainly easier to simply tell students what to do. Consider the following example of an obedience method and a choice method for a student who is talking out in class:

Obedience Method

Teacher: John, the rule is no talking.

Student gets quiet and talks out again.

Teacher: Be quiet.

Student gets quiet and talks out again.

Teacher: I told you to get quiet. The next time it's out you go.

Responsibility or Choice Method

Teacher: What is the rule about talking in our classroom? You may take notes or sit quietly during the lesson.

Student gets quiet and talks again.

Teacher: Are you making a good choice right now?

Student gets quiet and talks again.

Teacher   (semiprivately): What do you think will happen if you choose to continue this behavior? I know you can make a good choice.

In either example the behavior of the student could have continued or ceased. Obedience strategies can work; however, in these brief scenarios, which student did more critical thinking and decision making? Which strategy sends the message that the student has the power to make better choices? Which strategy would preserve the teacher-student relationship more effectively? Which strategy is more likely to escalate into a scene or power struggle? Which strategy was more instructional than punitive?

In the choice method notice the two choices that the teacher used (take notes or sit quietly) are both acceptable options. An effective choice is when the teacher can live with whichever one the student chooses. Teachers also should be careful to give reasonable choices. For example, the statement "You can stop talking or go to the office" is actually a threat hidden in a choice. Giving choices that the teacher can live with leads to a shared responsibility in the classroom. At an appropriate time the teacher can help the student examine the effectiveness of his or her choices (self-evaluate).

SELF-MANAGEMENT STRATEGIES

Self-management entails involving students in monitoring and controlling their own behavior. For students to control their own behavior they must have self-awareness and self-control, which are the building blocks of responsible behavior. These strategies reduce student dependence on the presence of an adult. Self-management has been successfully applied to improve on-task rate, academic productivity, academic accuracy, and social skills. At the heart of these self-management strategies is what is called self-monitoring. Self-monitoring involves keeping track of one's behavior. The act of self-monitoring alone has been shown to impact behavior (Algozzine & Ysseldyke, 1997).

Most self-management strategies involve training students or the entire class in self-monitoring (observing one's own behavior), self-recording (individual records or tallies the behavior), self-evaluation (comparison to some standard of effectiveness), and self-reinforcement (rewarding or praising oneself). Self-management strategies are especially effective when students have the appropriate behavior skill but lack self-awareness of their own behavior or in knowing when to exhibit the appropriate behavior. In addition, attempts to increase a desired behavior through self-management have been more effective than attempts to reduce an undesirable behavior (Goldstein, 1995). Most self-management programs consist of sequential steps, such as the following:

- *Selecting and practicing desirable behavior.* Again, it is important to remember to select a behavior to increase rather than one to decrease. For example, if the student were talking out in class, a more desirable behavior would be raising his or her hand before speaking. Students will need to know exactly what the desired behavior looks like. It is also best for them to practice the desired behavior as much as possible with the teacher prior to starting the program.

- *Selecting and practicing a method of self-recording.* Next, the teacher decides the best way for the student to self-record. There are generally three ways this can be done. The student can use frequency counts and tally when the behavior occurs on a designated sheet on his or her desk. An interval count involves the student being signaled at a certain time interval to record their behavior. For example, a cassette tape or kitchen timer could chime, which would signal the student to ask, "Was I on task?" The student would indicate a "+" or a "−" or a "yes" or "no" on a self-monitoring card or sheet. A third way to self-record is at the end of each class or subject period. Students need to practice recording before beginning the program. Some teachers like to record along with the student to ensure accuracy, especially at first. This practice can be faded out eventually once the student becomes more accurate.

- *Setting a goal and time lines for evaluation.* Next, the teacher and student design a behavioral goal and a time line for accomplishing the goal. For example, the teacher and student could decide to meet weekly to review progress and revise goals.

- *Planning for self-reinforcement.* The final step is for the teacher and student to plan the self-reinforcement. If the student shows improvement or moves closer to the goal at the end of each day or week, he or she may self-reinforce. Students may self-reinforce for accurate self-recording as well. Teachers may choose to provide a reward at the beginning of the program and gradually fade this out, replaced with the student using self-praise or self-reward.

Self-management strategies can be used with the entire class. Teachers can use a cue or signal, which cues the students to ask, "Am I doing what I am suppose to be doing?" Students could check their own behavior and record and compare their behavior to that on the previous day.

Algozzine and Ysseldyke (1997) suggest a technique where teachers place a small flagpole on their desk or somewhere visible to the entire class. If the teacher notices someone who is off task, he or she raises the flag. Students are told beforehand that this cue means to check your own behavior. Once the student or students are reengaged with the task at hand, the flag is lowered, and students may be congratulated for checking and changing their own behavior.

Another strategy called self-instruction is to cue the student to ask some or all of the following questions that are posted or listed on the student's desk:

- What am I supposed to be doing? Student states what the task at hand is.

- Do I have a plan? Student states a plan of attack.

- How am I doing? Student rates how the plan is working.

- Am I finished? Student checks to make sure work is completed.

- How did I do? Student rates effort that was put forth.

Teachers can model a task performance and ask these questions aloud. Next, students can perform the task while asking the questions. The goal is to get students to the point where they are whispering the questions and eventually subvocalizing or asking the questions inside their heads. This is also a useful strategy to use for academic tasks that require a sequence.

One final self-management strategy, which improves student responsibility in academic and homework areas, is to require them to keep a weekly summary sheet of all the learning activities and assignments and how many points each is worth. Students are also required to record the points they earned beside each activity or assignment. This sheet is kept in a notebook and must be signed daily or weekly by the parent. This strategy has many benefits. It keeps the child and parent informed of required work and provides feedback on academic and work progress. This strategy also helps students make the connection between effort and success or failure.

Self-management strategies increase the building blocks of responsibility, such as self-awareness, ownership, and self-control. Self-management strategies, by their very nature of involving students in recording, monitoring, and praising their own behavior, increase student responsibility.

WDEP SYSTEM OF CONVERSATION

One of the best techniques to increase student responsibility for change while preserving the relationship is the WDEP conversation or dialoguing technique, developed by Wubbolding (2000) as a delivery system of reality therapy. Each letter in WDEP stands for a concept: The *W* stands for wants, the *D* for doing, the *E* for self-evaluation, and the *P* for planning. When a student is displaying a pattern of ineffective behaviors, the responsibility-oriented teacher could engage the student in an action-plan or WDEP dialogue by asking the following questions, which can be used in verbal form for younger students and in either verbal or written form for older students:

1. *Wants (W):* What do you want? What do you want from teachers? Peers?

2. *Doing (D):* What are you doing to get what you want? In what direction is your behavior leading?

3. *Evaluation (E):* Is that helping you get what you want or hurting you?

4. *Planning (P):* Are you willing to try something different to get what you want?

Here is an example of a typical conference with a middle school student who was not doing his out-of-class assignments. This is followed by an example using the WDEP system of communication.

Example of a Typical System of Communication

Teacher: You are falling behind in your assignments. Your grade is really suffering.

Student: Yeah.

Teacher: If you do not turn those assignments in, they will turn to zeros.

Student: Yeah.

Teacher: Why haven't you gotten your work done?

Student: The assignments are boring.

Teacher: No one can do the assignments for you. You are responsible for them. Are you going to start doing your assignments?

Student: Yeah.

In this scenario the teacher and student remain on positive terms. However, many conversations between teachers or principals and students are much more coercive and obedience oriented. It is possible, even in this mild example, that the student may leave this interaction feeling that the teacher was on his case. In addition, responsibility comes from awareness, ownership or self-acceptance, self-control, self-evaluation, and planning more effective behavior. In this scenario, does the student become more aware of his own behavior? Does the student accept ownership of his behavior? Actually, it appears that the student fails to take responsibility since he blames his inability to finish work on the "boring" homework. When we confront students head on and when we ask "why" questions, they often respond with excuses that reduce ownership. Does the student self-evaluate his behavior or does the teacher evaluate the student's behavior? Is there any student planning for more effective behavior? While the student agrees with the plan that the teacher devised, there appears to be little or no ownership in the plan. Is it possible, he agrees just to get the teacher off his case? Do we tend to tell students what to do and why they should do it that way? Telling them what to do and why increases external control and obedience, not responsibility and self-control. Contrast this scenario with the following WDEP system of conversation.

Example of the WDEP System of Conversation

Teacher: I noticed you are getting behind in your work.

Student: Yep.

Teacher: What do you want to get out of this class? (*W* question)

Student: I'd like to get a decent grade, so my parents will get off my back.

Teacher: Is what you are doing helping you get a decent grade and getting your parents off your back? (*E* question)

Student: No, I guess not.

Teacher: What are you willing to do differently that might help? (*P* question)

Student: I could study more?

Teacher: Do you think that would help? (*E* question)

Student: I guess.

Teacher: How long would you say you have been studying each night? (*D* question)

Student: Fifteen minutes to a half hour.

Teacher: How long would you be willing to study to get your parents off your back? (*W* question)

Student: Until I get it done.

Teacher: Most students your age need to study about 1 hour and 15 minutes, depending on whether or not they have a test the next day.

Student: I would be willing to study for an hour but not for 1 hour and 15 minutes.

Teacher: Would you be willing to start tonight? (*P* question)

Student: Yeah.

Teacher: I'll be checking back with you to see if your plan is working.

Although the process doesn't always go as smoothly as in the example, some key points are revealed. How does this scenario differ from the first scenario? In the WDEP scenario, who is doing most of the evaluating? Is the student learning valuable decision-making skills and planning? Who takes more ownership for solving the problem, the teacher or student? Is the student learning self-awareness? Does the student have the opportunity to blame or diffuse responsibility? Is the teacher-student relationship preserved or even enhanced?

The reader will notice how many times the words *you* and *your* were used in the WDEP scenario. The use of these words sends the message that the student is capable of and responsible for making better choices and plans. In addition, the reader will notice that the teacher did not follow the WDEP system in exact sequence. It is not necessary to do so. The WDEP system is meant to be a guide and not an exact formula to follow.

It is very important that we do not succumb to the desire to create the action plan for the student. If confronted with a litany of "I don't know" answers to the questions, it is best to allow silence and repeat the question. If the student continues with this strategy, you could say, "Well what would you say if you did know?" It is more effective for the plan to come from the student, even if it is not what the teacher would have chosen. The aim for an action plan is for it to be student derived and need satisfying, without interfering with the needs of others in the classroom. Finally, this plan need not be magnificent. Any plan that moves the student in the right direction is a good start. Sometimes the best starter plans are when students just agree to think about something that was discussed.

It is essential to keep in mind that this system works most effectively after a caring and supportive relationship has been established. If trust is not established or the student is questioning your intent, they will not dialogue openly. However, just communicating with students in this way improves the teacher-student relationship. In addition, it is vital to remember that in communication only a very small percentage of the message sent to the other person is verbal. The majority of the message is determined by the tone of voice and body language of the communicator.

Finally, do not expect immediate results. Instead of focusing on immediate behavior change think about how these techniques influence your relationship with your students and how you feel about yourself after communicating in this fashion. Try not to get discouraged when students respond to these questioning techniques by saying, "I don't know." Many students have never been approached in this manner before, but once they see that it is safe, they will start to answer the questions. These techniques develop and preserve the relationship while increasing student responsibility for change. The following sections provide more examples of questions that one might use for each concept or letter in the WDEP system.

W Questions (Target what the student wants, how badly, and whether it is realistic)

- What do you want?

- What do you want from me?

- What do you want from the other students?
- What do you want from your parents?
- What do you want out of this class?
- How much are you willing to work to get it?
- Is what you want realistic?

D Questions (Target what the student is currently doing and the direction of behavior)

- What are you doing?
- What are you doing during study time?
- What are you doing right now?
- How long are you watching T.V.?
- What are you doing at home?
- What are you doing to make friends?

E Questions (Target asking the student about the effectiveness of his or her behavior)

- Is what you are doing helping or hurting you?
- Is that helping you get what you want?
- Is that helping you reach your goal?
- Are you going in the right direction to get what you want?
- Does it help you to look at things that way?
- Is that helping the class?
- Is that against the rules?

P Questions (Target assisting the student in devising a plan of action)

- What is your plan?
- Can you think of a better plan to help you get what you want?
- Can you think of a plan that would help you and our class?

- Are willing to think about a better plan?

- When will you do it?

- On a scale from 1 to 10 what are the chances of you carrying out your plan?

- Do you see any obstacles that might get in the way of completing your plan?

ACTION PLANNING AND GOAL SETTING

When students are aware of their behavior and have evaluated whether it is helping or hurting them, they are then able to devise a more helpful plan. When students participate in setting goals for their own behavior they feel more responsible for their behavior. Besides devising the plan for the student, other common errors include making grandiose plans and choosing the most difficult behavior to change. Plans can be as simple as getting the student to agree to think about something. For plans to be effective they need not be dramatic changes from what the student is already doing. Sometimes the best plans are when we can get the student to take a small step in the right direction. Any move in a more helpful or effective direction causes a ripple effect, possibly leading to more positive behaviors.

This section summarizes critical elements of action planning, or the *P* in the WDEP system. These elements will increase the likelihood that a goal or plan will be carried out successfully. Each component is followed by a positive example and a negative example. If you do not wish to engage in the WDEP system but wish to help students in setting and reaching goals, these ideas will be helpful. Action plans and goals are more likely to be accomplished if they meet the following criteria, adapted from Wubbolding (2000):

- *Simple.* The plan should be easily understood.

Positive example: I will write down all of my assignments each day.

Negative example: I will call my friends and ask them for the work.

- *Specific.* The details of what, where, when, and how are covered.

Positive example: I will write down all of my assignments in my assignment book, 5 minutes before the end of class.

Negative example: I will start writing my assignments down.

- *Realistic.* The plan is attainable under reasonable circumstances.

Positive example: I will write down all of my assignments in my assignment book.

Negative example: I will remember to do all of my assignments.

- *Observable and measurable.* The plan is observable and can be measured.

Positive example: I will greet my teacher and participate in at least one class discussion.

Negative example: I will be nicer to my teacher.

- *Dependent on the doer.* The success of the plan is not contingent on another person.

Positive example: I will write my assignments down.

Negative example: I will write my assignments down if my teacher reminds me to.

- *Positively stated.* The plan is what the student will start, not what the student will stop, doing.

Positive example: I will say nice things to my teacher.

Negative example: I will not criticize my teacher.

- *Process centered.* Details how the student will accomplish the plan.

Positive example: I will study one hour each night and extra for tests.

Negative example: I will get all A's on my report card.

- *Committed to.* The commitment to work on the plan is strong.

Positive example: I'll start greeting my teacher and participating today.

Negative example: I'll try to start my goal today.

SUMMARY OF MAIN POINTS

- It is easier to build obedience than it is to build responsibility in our students. Obedience, however, is short lived and requires the presence of an adult.

- Punishment often leads students to focus on the punishment, the punisher, and the negative feelings, instead of reflecting on their behavior and how they can make better choices in the future.

- The building blocks of responsibility are self-awareness, acceptance or ownership of one's behavior, self-evaluation of the effectiveness of one's behavior, and planning.

- Simply telling our students to be responsible is not enough. The building blocks and the skills need to be taught. Teachers need to set the stage for responsible student behavior by setting clear objectives, teaching and practicing procedures, being consistent, and providing rich amounts of feedback.

- We can improve student responsibility by giving choices, allowing students ample opportunities to practice and display responsible behavior, minimizing or eliminating punishment, using self-management strategies, and using the WDEP system of conversation.

- The *W* focuses on what the student wants, how badly he or she wants it, and whether it is realistic; the *D* focuses on what the student is doing presently; the *E* focuses on whether or not what they are doing is helping them get what they want; and the *P* focuses on devising a better plan.

QUESTIONS FOR DISCUSSION AND SELF-EVALUATION

1. Does your school and classroom allow all types of students to have opportunities to practice responsible behavior?

2. What are the practical advantages of having students who are responsible rather than students who are obedient?

3. What strategies does your school and classroom already practice that foster the building blocks of responsibility?

4. What are some advantages of using self-management strategies in the classroom?

5. How might an adult and a student feel differently after communicating with the WDEP system versus a typical conversation?

ACTION PLAN

As a result of something that I learned in this chapter I plan to (be specific in your answer):

_____

_____

_____

RECOMMENDED RESOURCES

Bodine, R., & Crawford, D. (1999). *Developing emotional intelligence: Behavior management and conflict resolution in schools.* Champaign, IL: Research Press. This book provides useful discussion strategies that foster student self-control, responsibility, and emotional intelligence.

Gootman, M. (2001). *The caring teacher's guide to discipline: Helping young students learn self-control, responsibility, and respect.* Thousand Oaks, CA: Corwin. This book provides useful classroom management ideas that lead to self-control and responsibility rather than to external control and obedience. The book provides positive strategies for problem solving and dealing with anger in the classroom.

Wubbolding, R. (1988). *Using reality therapy.* New York: Harper & Row. This book provides more intense discussion and case examples of the WDEP system of reality therapy.

PART II

Reactive Strategies

CHAPTER EIGHT

Creating and Implementing Effective Consequences

If a student doesn't know how to read, we teach.
If a student doesn't know how to swim, we teach.
If a student doesn't know how to multiply, we teach.
If a student doesn't know how to behave, we . . .
punish?

—John Herner
(quoted in McCart & Turnbull, 2002)

CHAPTER OBJECTIVES

In this chapter the reader will learn:

- How to use the seven criteria for effective consequences
- General considerations for responding to student behavior
- The core consequences of a relationship-driven classroom
- Preplanned response strategies to misbehavior

The strategies for developing a proactive classroom, establishing positive and personal relationships with your students, teaching and modeling prosocial skills, enhancing academic success and motivation, and building student responsibility will eliminate the majority of behavior problems in the classroom. Since the teacher has designed the classroom to satisfy the basic psychological needs of belonging, power, freedom, and fun, the students are less likely to engage in maladaptive or ineffective behaviors to satisfy their basic needs. The majority of students are choosing effective behaviors that do not infringe on the rights of others.

However, teachers will still need consequences or reactive measures to deal with the behaviors that arise in the typical classroom. It is critical to keep in mind that consequences alone will not eliminate all classroom problems. Consequences are more effective if accompanied by a positive classroom climate and positive and personal teacher-student relationships. Teachers should rely more on prevention than consequences in effective management of the classroom.

CONSEQUENCES IN WELL-MANAGED CLASSROOMS

In well-managed classrooms consequences are used sparingly but consistently when necessary. When consequences have to be used only occasionally, it is likely due to the teacher taking the time to prevent misbehavior by developing positive relationships, teaching procedural expectations and rules on a regular basis, teaching and modeling social-emotional skills, enhancing academic success and motivation, and building student responsibility. Bodine and Crawford (1999) state, "A consequence in and of itself will not change a behavior. A consequence only works when learners find value in the relationship with the person asking them to do something, or when they see value in what they are being asked to do" (p. 123). The most effective consequences, without the use of prevention strategies, are of little value.

Effective classroom managers prepare for the types of misbehavior they are likely to face and have numerous responses or strategies at their disposal to deal with the behaviors. This chapter focuses on the seven criteria for effective consequences and the relationship-driven core consequences. The next chapter discusses more strategies for dealing with and motivating difficult and resistant students. The classroom teacher is not limited to the consequences suggested in this chapter; instead, the relationship-driven approach advocates that we examine and take an inventory of the strategies in our discipline toolbox. In a relationship-driven classroom the teacher evaluates the consequences that are chosen in the classroom, using the following seven criteria for effective consequences:

1. Does the consequence bring the teacher and student closer together or create distance in the relationship?

2. Would this consequence encourage the teacher to change his or her own behavior?

3. Does the consequence and the way it is delivered model the prosocial skills that the teacher wants his or her students to possess?

4. Does the consequence instruct or teach appropriate behavior?

5. Does the consequence interfere with the flow of the lesson?

6. Does the consequence give the learner the choice to redirect and receive instruction?

7. Is the consequence effective?

Few consequences will meet all seven criteria, but the more criteria met, the more effective the consequence will be for short- and long-term change. Consequences such as these reduce misbehavior and lead to the development of resilience in students. They are positive and preventive because they are instructional and preserve the teacher-student relationship. Relationship-driven consequences help to create an environment typified by mutual respect, caring, responsibility, and cooperation. These criteria for evaluating consequences are not meant to undermine the confidence of the teacher in responding to misbehavior but are provided as a framework to help the classroom teacher evaluate the impact consequences may have on the teacher-student relationship. Before I discuss core consequences, a more thorough discussion of the seven criteria for effective consequences is necessary.

THE SEVEN CRITERIA
FOR EFFECTIVE CONSEQUENCES

Does the Consequence Bring the
Teacher and Student Closer Together?

We have already learned that the teacher-student relationship is critical and related to increased motivation, achievement, and resilience. A consequence that stops the misbehavior but hurts the teacher-student relationship is of little value. Since positive relationships are the top priority, consequences must not put distance or a wedge between the teacher and student. The consequences should not disturb the classroom climate. Some obvious negative examples include harsh punishments, yelling, lecturing, embarrassing, nagging, sarcasm, and exclusion. More subtle examples are consequences that cause the student to lose respect for the teacher, such as inconsistency, complaining, inducing guilt, or behaving like a martyr.

Consequences or interactions that breed resentment, anger, and disrespect may temporarily stabilize the behavior, but unfortunately they do not lead to long-term change, resilience, and optimal learning. When a student is dealt with harshly, he or she may become compliant, the cost of which can be student anger, resentment, embarrassment, fear, or even retaliation, which will interfere with learning. When anger and win-lose strategies (teachers win and students lose) characterize discipline interactions, relationships and classroom climate suffer. When relationships and climate suffer, cooperation, motivation, achievement, and resilience suffer as well. Do you respond to misbehavior in a way that places a wedge between you and your students?

Would the Consequence Encourage the
Teacher to Change His or Her Own Behavior?

This criterion is likely to be the most controversial of all. It asks you as the adult to reflect on how you would like a boss or manager to respond to you when you make a mistake. The next step is to look at how we respond to our students and determine if our response is similar or dissimilar to how we would want to be treated. Children may have different perceptual abilities than adults, but they have similar feelings.

Asking yourself how you would feel if someone used a particular consequence in response to your behavior is a question that is basic to empathy. Empathy is an important teacher character trait and also one we would like in our students. For example, let's say a student interrupts the teacher during class. The teacher responds with a statement such as, "Jonathon, how many times do I have to tell you to not interrupt me when I'm teaching? Go sit in the hall." How would you feel if someone you cared about said this or something similar to you in response to your interruption? How would you feel if you were attending a professional development seminar and the presenter responded to you in this fashion?

Why is it acceptable to talk to students in a way that we would not talk to our friends or we would not like to be talked to ourselves? Do our students deserve less than what we would want for ourselves? In the previous example, an alternative response could be "Jonathon, remind us of the rule about talking when someone else is talking" or "Jonathon, it is pretty frustrating when you talk when I am talking. I'll wait until you're finished." Would these statements encourage you to change your behavior? Which ones would you prefer as a consequence for your own behavior? Do the consequences and the manner in which they are delivered in your classroom reflect how you would like to be treated?

Do the Consequence and the Way It Is Delivered Model the Prosocial Skills You Want the Students to Possess?

This criterion focuses on modeling. Modeling is a critical strategy in changing the behavior of students. If we wish our students to display patience, for example, then we must be patient with them. If we want our students to be effective problem solvers, then we must model effective problem solving. When misbehavior disturbs the classroom, the teacher, in fact, has a problem. How the teacher responds to this disturbance sends a powerful message to the students about how to handle conflict and problems. Students observe the manner in which teachers handle stress, disappointment, mistakes, anger, and conflict with other adults and students.

Positive modeling is especially important when we are angry. How do we wish our students to behave when they are angry? Do we expect them to get loud, lash out, or display a temper tantrum? Ideally we want our students to be able to calm down, discuss their feelings, and find a solution. How do we behave toward our students when we are angry? We exhibit poor modeling when we say that they should handle their anger in one way, but then we do not handle our anger in a similar fashion. To make matters worse students seem to have some sort of built-in radar to notice when we are not practicing what we preach. Are you routinely modeling the behaviors you want to see your students display?

Does the Consequence Teach Appropriate Behavior?

A consequence that does not teach alternate or replacement behaviors is essentially punishment. The goal of a consequence is to increase appropriate behavior over the long term, whereas the goal of punishment is to suppress misbehavior. Effective discipline involves teaching and practicing more effective behaviors for the future. Consequences that teach and encourage a more desirable behavior are called corrective consequences.

Instructional or corrective consequences are the rule rather than the exception in a relationship-driven classroom. In an environment like school, where the goal is to instruct, one would expect behavior to be fair game as well. However, behavior falls under the myth of assumed skill. In other words, we tend to assume that students understand the expectation, are aware of their own behavior, and are capable of choosing a more effective behavior. The first conclusion a teacher should reach when confronted with misbehavior is that the student may lack understanding of the expectations and needs more practice. In other words, the student needs more practice to follow the rule.

If a student loses his or her temper in class, some noninstructional consequences would be to send the student to the office, give detention, or tell the student to calm down. Obviously the student may not know how to calm down. Certainly a detention or trip to the office would not teach alternate behaviors. A corrective consequence might be to bring the student aside and say, "Let's try to take some deep breaths, so we can think this problem out." At a later time you might help the student come up with a plan for alternatives to outbursts in class. For younger students, you might want to develop a plan that teaches students to recognize their increased anger and to ask for help. At a later time it may be helpful to have the student practice an alternate, replacement, or incompatible behavior to outbursts. A replacement behavior is a newly shaped behavior that meets a need for a child in a more effective manner than does the misbehavior. For example, a replacement behavior for arguing is asking questions in a calm way or writing a note. The student still gets to communicate and be heard but in a more appropriate manner, time, and place. An incompatible behavior is usually a positive or prosocial behavior that can't exist at the same time as a negative behavior. You might arrange for the student to practice relaxation or calming strategies, so the student has these techniques at their disposal the next time he or she feels like losing control. Anger and relaxation are incompatible because they cannot coexist together easily. Keep in mind it is easier to increase behavior than it is to decrease behavior (Goldstein, 1995). In other words, plan for students to do something more appropriate rather than stop doing something inappropriate.

Whenever you are tempted to use a consequence or intervention to get a student to stop or decrease a certain behavior, instead pick a replacement or incompatible behavior to increase. If you want a student to decrease bullying behaviors, then try to increase nonaggressive behavior. Teach students to increase raising their hand prior to speaking rather than focusing on getting students to stop talking. Target increasing on-task behavior (work productivity) rather than trying to decrease off-task behavior. Self-evaluate by asking yourself if your consequences teach or allow for practice of a more desirable alternative behavior.

Does the Consequence Interfere With the Flow of the Lesson?

Ideally, a consequence should allow the teacher and class to get back to business with little or no interference. Consequences for misbehavior should involve the least amount of time and effort, unpleasant feelings, and disruption to learning (Evertson & Harris, 2003). Effective teachers use less intrusive techniques as much as possible, such as proximity, eye contact, a look, a cue, a gentle touch on the elbow, or subtle gesture or comment to continue the momentum of the lesson. Ideally, the teacher should use the least intrusive consequences possible to redirect student behavior before it escalates. If the teacher responds with the most intrusive consequences at the first sign of misbehavior, classroom climate, relationships, and flow will be hampered. When these techniques are not successful at redirecting behavior, the teacher will have to break the lesson flow by reminding the student of the rule, asking a brief question, requesting a specific behavior, or giving some other consequence.

Teachers who willingly or unwillingly are baited into power struggles with students violate this criterion. Power struggles hurt lesson momentum and classroom atmosphere. Since most power struggles end with the teacher punishing or threatening to punish, negative emotions are evoked not only from the parties involved but also from the rest of the class. Since students are experiencing enhanced stress, they are not in an optimal learning mode.

A cardinal rule for dealing with power struggles is to avoid them since no one wins and the entire class is penalized. The best way to avoid a power struggle or argument is to avoid giving ultimatums, acknowledge strong emotions, use levity or humor, and buy time. For example, if a student defiantly refuses to do something you ask, you might say, "You seem pretty upset right now. Maybe we could talk about this after the lesson." If a student tries to argue, you might say, "I am glad you feel comfortable enough to share such strong feelings, but we will have to talk about them later," or respond with, "Well I see things differently." All these responses make it difficult to argue back.

Many teachers panic when dealing with open defiance or some other power play. They believe that the other students will learn that they too can get away with this type of behavior. They feel they must use all the power at their disposal or risk chaos. In reality, the majority of students in a typical classroom will not copy the defiant behavior. Ironically, losing your cool or making an example of this student can in some cases increase future misbehavior. Students sometimes enjoy the power in being able to make adults lose their temper. An effective technique to buy time and avoid a power struggle is to say, "I'm going to have to do something about that, but right now I am busy teaching." Do not mistake avoiding the power struggle and buying some time as a sign of weakness. The student can be dealt with when emotions are calmer; the lesson and atmosphere are preserved, and the other students are not penalized. Do you let students detract from the academic lesson by baiting you into power struggles? Do you exhaust the least intrusive strategies to redirect behavior before breaking the lesson flow? Do you intervene early in the sequence of misbehavior before it escalates?

Does the Consequence Give the Learner the Choice to Redirect and Receive Instruction?

The importance of choices cannot be overemphasized when confronting misbehavior. Allowing choice, both positive and negative, increases responsibility and inner control. Giving choices has the added benefits of preserving the relationship, increasing ownership, and reducing resentment. Giving choices also sends a clear message that the teacher believes the student is able to make more effective choices.

Using choices has another important advantage over traditional consequences or just telling the person to stop whatever he or she is doing. By offering a choice, the teacher is usually instructing in more appropriate alternate behaviors at the same time. For example, the teacher may state, "You can choose to get back to work or choose to have more work to take home tonight" or "You can work on your science or mathematics. The choice is yours." Contrast these statements with "Stop fooling around!" The first set of statements give the student a positive alternative to what they are doing instead of simply telling the student what to stop doing. This strategy also helps satisfy the criterion for effective consequences to teach alternate behaviors.

Be careful not to hide your choice in criticism. For example, "If you spent more time working and less time talking, you might get somewhere." Also, remember a good choice gives two viable alternatives, both of which are acceptable to the teacher. Try not to hide your punishments or threats under the guise of using choices, such as, "Stop talking or go to the office. It's your choice."

Now I move to the second part of this criterion—receive instruction. It is counterproductive to use a consequence that ends the misbehavior but, because of its nature, blocks the student's ability to process information clearly and effectively. If the student feels threatened, embarrassed, angry, anxious, stressed, or fearful, learning will be hindered. There is also a good chance that if one student is feeling strong emotions than so are other students in the classroom. Under high emotion, the brain takes on a defensive posture and reduces the ability of the student to do higher-order thinking or learning (Goleman, 1995). A common example is when a student who appears to be off-task or daydreaming is called on purposefully to catch the student not knowing where the rest of the class is in the lesson. This consequence will temporarily bring the student back on task only to feel embarrassed. A better alternative would be to call on or acknowledge a nearby student. If you do call on the daydreaming student, review the question and then ask for a response. When students are embarrassed, they are not in a good state to receive information and learn.

Is the Consequence Effective?

Does the consequence work? This seems so obvious that one would wonder why it is included in the criteria for effective consequences. However, we often continue using consequences despite evidence of their ineffectiveness. This is often the case with punishment. Many times students continue to receive punishment, regardless of whether or not it is reducing the problem behavior. At times their misbehavior is suppressed only to reemerge later. We then respond with more intense punishment, a dangerous and counterintuitive cycle. We may do this because we lack alternative strategies or just because we fail to self-evaluate by asking, "Is this helping?" We may also continue with punitive consequences because society tells us that to change students they must experience pain. As educators we should strive for long-term change not just temporary stabilization. In the relationship-driven classroom the effectiveness of consequences is determined by their long-term effectiveness and their effect on the teacher-student relationship.

It is critical to make sure you give your interventions adequate time to make an impact. Most consequences for behavior lead to an initial increase in the target behavior. In other words, the behavior usually gets worse before it gets better. On the other hand, if you have given a strategy adequate time to test, then it may be time to try something else. Ideally, determining the effectiveness of consequences will be accompanied by some pre- and postdata. Predata, or baseline data, are collected prior to starting an intervention or strategy, and postdata are collected after the intervention has begun. The teacher, student, aide, consultant, principal, or support staff can collect behavioral data.

Data usually provide information about the behavior in terms of how much, how often, and how long it occurs. The most common form of data is frequency or how often the behavior occurs. This can be determined by tallying the number of times the student talks out, fights, or swears, for example. The intensity, or how much of the behavior is evident, is the most difficult to measure. For example, the intensity of a tantrum would require some subjectivity to measure. Academic behaviors, like productivity, can be measured for intensity by just counting the number of problems completed. The duration of behavior, or how long it occurs, requires timing the length of time the student waits to get started on work or how long a student's tantrum lasts, for example.

Objective data are helpful because we all sometimes misperceive situations, especially when our emotions are running high. Data often help both teacher and student view the behavior more objectively. Data also help with decision making for referrals for special education and for communicating with parents about the nature and severity of the problem. One way to build student self-awareness and self-control and to obtain data is to have the student keep track of his or her behaviors. Self-monitoring and recording were discussed in the previous chapter. Data give you a benchmark to determine the effectiveness of the new consequences and interventions and can also be a source of motivation for students. Showing students visually how they are improving can be a very powerful strategy. For example, one teacher measured words per minute that a student was able to read and graphed the results, which showed the steady improvements. The student checked the data chart weekly and was motivated to keep improving. Many education software packages use data and graphing to increase motivation. Collecting data can also enhance teacher motivation—we can see some evidence that our work is paying off.

RELATIONSHIP-DRIVEN CORE CONSEQUENCES

Core consequences are used for the majority of the behaviors in the typical classroom. The consequences are listed in order of intensity. This does not imply that the teacher must follow a particular order when using these consequences. The teacher can decide which consequence or combination of consequences is warranted for a particular situation. The reader will notice certain themes in the core consequences, such as questioning instead of commanding and allowing choice, student input, self-evaluation, and planning.

Self-evaluation is a key to long-term behavior change, self-awareness, responsibility, and better decision making and involves the students judging the effectiveness of their own behavior. Teachers can assist students in the self-evaluation process by asking questions such as "Is your behavior helping you get what you want?" or "Is your behavior helping or hurting others around you?" The 20 preplanned responses to misbehavior, which are discussed later in this chapter, provide more examples of teacher comments that prompt student self-evaluation. Teachers should try to avoid judging the behavior of the student. There is a tremendous difference between a student coming to the conclusion that the behavior he or she is exhibiting is not helping them get what they want and another person telling the student that the behavior is not helping or wrong. When someone else judges our behavior, most of the time our first response is to become defensive. When we ask students to self-evaluate, they are less defensive and able to take a more honest look at what they are doing.

Wubbolding (2000) states, "It is categorically impossible for human beings to make changes until they first decide that a change would be more advantageous" (p. 145). Students develop responsibility by evaluating their own behavior, making a plan for improvement, and carrying out the plan. When students are able to develop a plan for improvement and follow through with it on their own, responsibility, self-control, self-efficacy, problem-solving skills, and self-pride are enhanced. If students are simply told what to do, compliance and obedience are developed.

Relationship-driven consequences complement and build important social-emotional competencies (e.g., problem solving, critical thinking, self awareness, self-efficacy). In addition, and most important, these strategies preserve the teacher-student relationship. Although many of these consequences have been validated with research, teacher feedback reveals a more interesting result: Teachers who use these techniques state that they feel better about themselves than they do when they use more coercive, negative, or confrontational corrective strategies with students. The relationship-driven core consequences include effective cueing and signaling; precorrection; reteach and practice; preplanned responses; verbal plan of improvement (VPI); owe time plus VPI; responsibility action plan (RAP), with or without parent signature; and removal to a prearranged classroom or the office.

Effective Cueing and Signaling

When one student or a group of students is not following a rule, an effective first intervention (unless the behavior in question is serious or dangerous) is usually a look, gesture, cue, or signal. For example, effective teachers use proximity and eye contact as a signal to misbehaving students. Other effective teachers use cues and signals to gain the attention of the class. A teacher may use a hand signal, counting, or classroom lights as cues for students to redirect their attention and get quiet.

The hand signal has some advantages over the other signals. This technique is most effective if the teacher gives a short statement, such as "Class, attention please," followed by raising his or her hand. Students respond by stopping what they are doing and also raising their hands. Other students who did not hear the verbal prompt will respond when they see the other students with their hands up. This can be done outside the classroom as well (hallways, cafeteria, field trips, etc.). Using the lights as a signal may not be as convenient since the teacher may have to move to get to the switch and will not always have access to this as a signal (Sprick et al., 1998). Signals should be appropriate for the grade level of the students. Older students may resent signals like turning the lights off when they need to get quiet. However, older students still require signals, especially in classrooms that use group work or change learning formats often.

In addition to this whole-class method of signaling, individual students will need signals or cues to redirect their behavior. There are some students who are genuinely unaware of their own behavior. A cue may serve as a prompt or as a warning. These signals are effective means of increasing students' self-awareness. Students who daydream, hum, or tap their fingers on their desks may benefit from prearranged signals that mean to stop the behavior. Placing your hand on the student's desk or shoulder could serve as a signal to redirect behavior.

Precorrection

Precorrection is an underused strategy that involves preparing a student prior to going into a situation where misbehavior has occurred in the past. A teacher might remind the student of the behavior expectations, have the student repeat the behavioral expectations back to the teacher, allow practice, and discuss consequences that might follow any misbehavior. For example, a student who has difficulty at recess could be pulled aside prior to leaving. The teacher could state, "We will be going outside for recess. I will need you to keep your feet to yourself. What do you think will happen if you do not keep your feet to yourself?" After the student responds, the teacher could add, "I know you can do it." Precorrections work well for students who have difficulty with their behavior during transitions. One strategy that uses the idea of precorrection is thanking the student for a desired behavior before it is displayed (Curwin & Mendler, 1999a); for example, before taking a restroom break, the teacher could say, "Thank you for keeping your hands to yourself when we go to the restroom." This states the desired behavior beforehand, and students are more likely to comply with a request once they have been thanked in advance.

Reteach and Practice

The entire class needs to be taught expectations for behavior and specific classroom procedures throughout the school year. Many times adults do not realize how many subskills or sequential steps are required in typical classroom procedures. For example, the procedure for simply lining up to leave the classroom has approximately eight steps: Students have to put their materials away, wait for a cue, stand up, quietly push their chairs in, walk appropriately, maintain personal space, keep hands ,and feet to self, and wait for a cue to leave the room. In reteach and practice individual students relearn and practice following the rule or procedure that they are having difficulty following. The intent is for this to be an instructional time when students learn and practice the rule, similar to learning and practicing a mathematics computation, for example. Teachers would first teach and demonstrate, followed by student practice, feedback, and more practice until mastery is demonstrated.

Teachers must use caution to not turn this consequence into a punishment. Techniques such as requiring students to write their name 100 or more times if they forget to write their name on their papers and writing 500-word essays are not positive or instructional. I do not advocate such practices in part because these approaches can be very punitive (especially to those students with fine motor or other written expression disabilities), and other less punitive approaches are at least as effective. Our first conclusion when students are not following the rules should be that they need more practice.

Teaching and practicing rules are excellent logical consequences (related to the infraction) for students. Behaviors that respond well to teaching and practicing are independent seatwork, transition behavior, listening and following directions, and most any classroom procedure or transition. For example, if a student is having trouble handling transitions, the teacher could arrange a time to review and teach the behavioral expectations and have the student demonstrate mastery either verbally or behaviorally, or preferably both. Students who have trouble following directions could receive instruction and practice in making eye contact with the speaker, focusing on the words, rehearsing or repeating the directions silently, asking for needed clarification, and beginning the task.

Preplanned Responses

Having preplanned responses to predicted student behaviors can be very effective. Predicting the most likely misbehaviors of your students and rehearsing how you might respond can improve your confidence and effectiveness and help ensure that responses are delivered in a calm, efficient, and consistent manner. Preplanned responses are not designed to undermine teacher spontaneity and confidence but to increase the likelihood that the responses are relationship preserving. When confronted with behavior, we want to respond in a timely fashion and not always second-guess whether or not our responses are right or wrong.

One strategy is using a brief preplanned question or statement in response to misbehavior. Many times this question is rhetorical and need not be formally answered aloud by the student. If students are required to answer these questions, lesson flow will be affected. The questions are designed to elicit self-awareness, problem solving, critical thinking, and decision making in the entire class. An ideal scenario would be if the prompts or questions elicit some self-reflection by the student on the appropriateness of the behavior, and this alone would lead to self-redirection with little or no interference to lesson flow. For example, a teacher response to a student who is disturbing others might be "What is the rule about how we treat other people?" If necessary, a follow-up question might be "What could you do differently?"

These responses are not time consuming and will not hinder lesson momentum, classroom climate, or teacher-student relationships. The following is a list of 20 preplanned or rehearsed responses to misbehavior. Many of the responses are adapted specifically for teachers from reality therapy and the WDEP delivery system (Wubbolding, 2000). Some of the responses or questions can be used in private conferences as well as in front of the entire class. The questions and responses vary in directness since some students require a more direct approach. Teachers who are dealing with chronic misbehavior should also preplan a consequence if the response or question doesn't redirect the student's behavior. These responses can be adapted to fit your personal style. This list is meant to be a starting point.

One caution when dealing with a student's behavior or actions—avoid the use of "why" questions. "Why" questions elicit defensiveness and excuses and usually are answered with the phrase "I don't know." In the following examples, even if the student doesn't answer or responds with "I don't know," the connection is preserved and the student is prompted to self-evaluate. Please keep in mind the importance of eye contact, proximity, sincerity, and tone of voice when delivering responses to behavior. Even the most positive statement can be spoiled by an irritated or negative tone of voice. Also, certain students require more privacy than others in dealing with their behavior. Students who need to save face in front of their peers should be dealt with in private as much as possible.

Twenty Positive Preplanned Responses to Misbehavior

1. "[Student's name], please tell me the class rule on [state general idea of rule]."

2. "What happens if a student chooses to [state misbehavior]?"

3. "Can I count on you to [state rule or behavior to be followed]?"

4. "When can I expect you to start [state behavior you desire to see]?"

5. "Is there a better choice you can make right now?"

6. "Is what you are doing helping you be a successful student?"

7. "Is what you are doing helping or hurting the class?"

8. "When you [state behavior], does that help or hurt you in [list desired goal]?"

9. "What do you think will happen if you continue to [state behavior]?"

10. "I expect you to [state detailed behavior you desire]."

11. "I need you to [state detailed behavior you desire]."

12. "What did we agree would happen the next time you chose to [state behavior]?"

13. "You may try again tomorrow, but today you will need to [state consequence]."

14. "What do you think would be a fair consequence for you choosing to [state behavior]?"

15. "Is there a better choice you could make to meet your goal of [state predetermined goal of the student]?"

16. "It seems as if you may need my help to [list desired behavior]. Let's meet after class to discuss this further."

17. "We will have to discuss this behavior, but right now we have to get back to the lesson."

18. "Would you choose that behavior if you thought about it carefully?"

19. "You appear to need some time to calm down. Go back to [name the conflict corner or designated area of the classroom]."

20. "Please report to [state designated area in another teacher's room or time out area] until you have a plan to improve your behavior."

Verbal Plan of Improvement (VPI)

A VPI can be as simple as a one-sentence plan that is developed by the student and states what the student will do differently in the future. Ideally, a VPI will be specific, realistic, brief, and stated in the positive. In other words, the student states what he or she will do rather than what he or she will not do. It is imperative that the student state his or her plan and make a commitment to following it. Keep in mind that thinking of their own plan may be difficult at first since students are accustomed to the adult just telling them what to do differently. Most VPIs will begin with the phrase "I will." A simple example of a VPI would be for a student who has been bothering another student to say, "I will keep my hands to myself." VPIs can also address what needs to be done to make amends, rectify, or correct a wrong that was committed toward someone or something.

Owe Time Plus VPI

Requiring a student to lose time away from something they value (e.g., between classes with friends, recess, free time, after school) is often an effective consequence. When a student misbehaves in class, the teacher and the class lose time. Asking them to pay for that wasted time is logical. The amount of time owed can even be the same as the time wasted and does not have to be long. For example, holding a middle or high school student back just 30 seconds from their friends in the hallway can be enough. The teacher must decide how much time the student owes and what they will do during this time. The student could do a VPI during this time.

Be careful that this time does not become discussion or relationship-building time. These should take place at other times when the student does not owe time. There are two scenarios when I do not recommend this strategy. The first is when a student is avoiding socialization or seems to enjoy owing time. The second is when you find that a student is missing out on many opportunities to socialize or blow off steam.

Responsibility Action Plan (RAP)

When a student is displaying ineffective behaviors, the responsibility-oriented teacher engages the student in action planning or goal setting. The RAP is for older students and consists of completing the RAP Worksheet (younger students could fill out this sheet with some assistance). The teachers have a choice of whether they would like a parent signature on the completed RAP Worksheet. This worksheet consists of three questions (see Figure 8.1). These questions are just a short version of the WDEP system of conversation from the last chapter. Notice that these three questions use language that sends the message that the student is choosing the behaviors and that the student is responsible for changes. This process reduces excuse making, which is common when we ask students about their behavior. In addition, since this form is signed by all parties it acts as a behavior contract.

Removal to a Prearranged Classroom

Many teachers have had success using this strategy. In this strategy a student is removed and sent to a prearranged, nearby

Figure 8.1   Responsibility Action Plan (RAP)

RAP Worksheet

1. What specifically were you doing in class?

2. Are the choices you are making helping or hurting your success in this class?

3. What could you agree to do differently today or tomorrow? Please be specific.

Student Signature: _____
Teacher Signature: _____
Parent Signature: _____

classroom for a designated time period. In other words, the receiving teacher knows and agrees in advance that this will happen. The rationale for this strategy is that the student is less likely to act out in a different class, especially if the students of the receiving classroom have been instructed to ignore the student. The student could work on an RAP during this removal and should not be allowed back into class without an agreed-on plan for improvement. I do not recommend sending a student to a grade level much lower because this will be humiliating for the student. One caution is that any technique that removes a student from his peers and away from the curriculum should be used sparingly. Overuse of this consequence can send the message that problems are solved by pushing out rather than talking them out. If this consequence has been used more than a few times without success, discontinue and seek assistance.

Removal to the Office

Removal to the office should only be used in cases of dangerous behavior or if prearranged with the principal. There are more behavior problems in schools where teachers expect most discipline issues to be handled by the administrator (Hawkins, Doueck, & Lishner, 1988). This practice can undermine the authority of the teacher and relinquishes control to the principal. Once you send a student to the principal, you have to accept his or her decision on how to best handle the situation. Ideally teachers and principals should work collaboratively in dealing with discipline problems. There should be a clear understanding of which behaviors the teacher will handle and which the principal will handle. Generally speaking, teachers should immediately refer cases of stealing, fighting, verbal and physical harassment, and vandalism to the administrator.

SUMMARY OF MAIN POINTS

- Consequences without prevention and relationship-building measures are of little long-term value.

- Relationship-driven teachers examine their responses to misbehavior using the seven criteria of effective consequences. Effective consequences lead to long-term behavior change, model important skills for students, model how the teacher would like to be treated, teach more effective behaviors, maintain the flow of instruction, allow for choice and problem solving, and preserve the teacher-student relationship.

- It is often more effective to teach a more effective alternative or incompatible behavior than to focus on decreasing misbehavior.

- Relationship-driven core consequences build self-awareness, cooperation, responsibility, and problem-solving and decision-making skills while preserving the teacher-student relationship and reducing alienation.

- Preplanned responses to misbehavior can improve teacher confidence and prompt the student to self-evaluate, problem solve, and redirect his or her own behavior.

QUESTIONS FOR
DISCUSSION AND SELF-EVALUATION

1. Name three common misbehaviors that occur in the classroom. Name a replacement or incompatible behavior for each one.

2. How can a teacher intervene or respond to the first signs of misbehavior without interfering with the lesson flow?

3. How do the consequences that are typically used in your school or classroom measure up in terms of the seven criteria for effective consequences?

4. What are some potential drawbacks of calling on parents or administrators to deal with classroom misbehavior?

5. Does your tone of voice, delivery, and consequences that you use with your students reflect how you would like to be treated if you made a mistake?

ACTION PLAN

As a result of something that I learned in this chapter I plan to (be specific in your answer):

_____

_____

_____

RECOMMENDED RESOURCES

Cummings, C. (2000). *Winning strategies for classroom management*. Alexandria, VA: Association for Supervision and Curriculum Development. This book is an excellent resource for teachers who are interested in teaching the skills that students need to succeed academically, socially, and behaviorally.

Curwin, R., & Mendler, A. (1999a). *Discipline with dignity*. Alexandria, VA: Association for Supervision and Curriculum

Development. This book discusses strategies that reduce misbehavior, increase responsibility and self-control, and preserve the dignity of the student.

Evertson, C., Emmer, E., & Worsham, M. (2003). *Classroom management for elementary teachers* (6th ed.). Boston: Allyn & Bacon. This book provides an excellent discussion on types and drawbacks of consequences that can be used in the classroom.

CHAPTER NINE

Building Relationships With Difficult and Resistant Students

"If we want to work effectively with difficult students, we must be willing to change ourselves."

—Richard Curwin and Allen Mendler (1999b, p. 25)

CHAPTER OBJECTIVES

In this chapter the reader will learn:

- Three common errors we make in dealing with difficult students
- Common ineffective beliefs of difficult students
- Strategies for challenging the ineffective beliefs of difficult students
- Nontraditional relationship-building strategies to use with difficult students
- The purpose, philosophy, and terminology involved in behavior support planning

This chapter is about rethinking some of our assumptions about dealing with difficult students and adding some nontraditional strategies to our toolbox for dealing with them. If we are going to gain the trust and cooperation of difficult and resistant students, we must rethink traditional methods of dealing with them. This chapter examines some common errors we make in dealing with difficult students, ineffective beliefs of difficult students and strategies for challenging those beliefs, relationship building with difficult students, and how to develop a behavior support plan for them.

THREE COMMON ERRORS IN DEALING WITH DIFFICULT STUDENTS

I believe we make three critical errors in our assumptions about dealing with difficult students: relying too heavily on punitive strategies, targeting too many behaviors to change, and ignoring exceptions to the problem behavior. All of these errors involve assumptions about what these students need and what solutions will be most effective.

Overreliance on Punitive Strategies

The first error stems from the tendency to resort to punitive measures with difficult students. Unfortunately, punishment is our first line of intervention, despite its history of ineffectiveness. The majority of these students have a history of behavior problems for which they were punished at home, at school, or both. If punishments were a solution, then they would have worked before. It seems that some well-meaning educators believe that even though punishment has failed in the past, the next punishment will take.

The punishment model may lead to compliance for some of these difficult students; however, for the majority of difficult students punishment only succeeds at alienating them and disconnecting them from significant adults at school. In the relationship-driven classroom the first line of intervention is not punishment but employing strategies to improve the relationship with the student. Interestingly, punitive strategies may be more effective for typical students than for difficult students (Sprick et al., 1998). Difficult students require a more positive relationship-oriented approach. When we are dealing with individual students, we need to ask ourselves if another punishment is really going to make a positive difference, especially since many of these difficult students have already experienced more severe punishments than schools would morally and ethically dispense.

Targeting Too Many Behaviors for Change

The second critical error we make in dealing with difficult students is our assumption that big problems require big solutions. Sometimes big changes take place as a result of a seemingly miniscule intervention (Kottler, 2002). Small changes can have a ripple effect and lead to more significant changes. Once again, with good intentions, we target too many behaviors, set unrealistic goals, or target the biggest and most challenging behaviors for change. This sometimes continues a cycle of failure and frustration for the difficult student. A better strategy is to encourage the student to commit to and to make small changes that lead to a better overall behavioral direction.

When working on a plan for change with the student, you might agree on one small and attainable goal. This goal can be as simple as asking the student to think about something. One example could be to ask, "Since we have to spend so much time together, would you think about what I could do to help us get along better?" Sometimes I ask students, "What is one thing you could do today to make this problem better?" Typical answers to this question are "I'll do all my homework" or "I'll stop getting in trouble." Many times students will state a goal that is unrealistic to please the adult or to get the adult off their case. They may tell you what they think you want to hear or maybe what has satisfied adults in the past. It is critical that we actually negotiate a more reasonable goal with the student. However, it is not necessary to tell them that they can't accomplish what they say they will. When a student states what seems to be an unrealistic goal, you may respond with a statement such as "I would be happy if you just did part of your assignment tonight, but if you choose to do the whole thing, then that is great too." If they do more, then everybody is happy. If they only do part of the assignment, that is still more than was completed before and is a step in the right direction. Remember, your goal is for the student to begin to realize that they can make more effective choices no matter how small or seemingly insignificant.

Ignoring Exceptions

The third error we make in dealing with difficult students is to overlook their personal interests, strengths, and exceptions to the problem behaviors. Exceptions to the problem are times when the problems are less evident or absent. When we are dealing with a student with chronic misbehavior, it can be very useful to examine when during the day the problems are less evident. Sometimes we are so programmed to study the problem and identify deficits that we forget to recognize and capitalize on students' strengths and exceptions, which can foster resilience.

Many difficult students have unique and extraordinary abilities. Unfortunately, many times these interests or strengths are unrelated to classroom curricular goals. One middle school math teacher decided to capitalize on a student's mechanical strength. This particular student had a reading disability but had extraordinary skills in mechanics. This teacher enlisted the student's help in fixing his broken lawnmowers and other mechanical items. This strategy did not help his grades, but his behavior and attitude were much improved.

Another useful area of inquiry when dealing with difficult and resistant students is in searching for exceptions to the problem. It is rare to find a student who displays equal amounts of inappropriate behavior across all subjects and teachers. Observations conducted throughout the day and across different settings can give us a picture not only of when problems typically arise but also of when and with whom problems are surprisingly absent. It can be helpful to inquire with the students about what they are doing differently in those situations and encourage them to do more of this exception behavior. Similarly, you may inquire about a time in the past when the problems were not as significant and ask, "What were you doing differently then?" The following case of Troy illustrates the potential of looking for exceptions.

Troy was a sixth grader who carried labels of severely emotionally disturbed and attention deficit hyperactivity disorder. At his mother's request Troy was being mainstreamed, or included in a regular education math, science, and social studies class. He received small-group instruction in reading and language arts. Troy was frequently in trouble, seldom did homework, and was failing all of his academic subjects. He had difficulty keeping his hands to himself and often swore at his peers and teachers. The typical strategies of trips to the office, phone calls home, and suspensions were not successful.

A meeting was called as Troy was on the verge of being sent to another school that housed a unit for students with behavior disorders. The principal, two regular education teachers, and a special education teacher described his behaviors and performance. After the meeting, it struck me as interesting that one of his regular education teachers reported that Troy completed 75% of his homework and had received no office referrals. I decided to pursue this exception by doing some classroom observations.

After observing Troy across settings, it became evident to me that his behavior was much worse in his special education classes than in his regular education class. If I had not already known this student, I would not have been able to identify him as a student with behavior problems during these observations. I decided to meet with Troy and inquire about these exceptions. He stated that he did not like being in the special education room because his friends made fun of him. I had heard this response many times before from other students. My typical response would be that if the student wanted to get out of special education, then the student must earn his or her way out into mainstream or regular classes. This time the team agreed to elaborate and extend the exception. His parents and teachers were willing to take a risk. The team agreed to remove him from his special education classes and place him in regular classes with tutoring assistance and a behavior contract. Troy still exhibited behavioral difficulties, but overall his office referrals decreased, his grades improved, and he was able to stay in his home school.

INEFFECTIVE BELIEFS OF DIFFICULT AND RESISTANT YOUTH

Difficult student behavior can often be traced to lack of appropriate social or behavioral skills, frustrated and unmet needs, and ineffective beliefs. Since we have already addressed teaching social-emotional skills and need satisfaction in earlier chapters, my focus in this section is on ineffective beliefs. Difficult students need a trusting and personal relationship with a teacher who can challenge their ineffective belief systems, which are not helpful and are often illogical or irrational. These ineffective beliefs are also called cognitive distortions, faulty beliefs, and self-defeating beliefs. Our beliefs influence our behavior and our emotions. It is very important to remember that difficult students may act in a way that is counterintuitive to adults but often makes sense in terms of their ineffective or faulty belief systems. Difficult students may unconsciously or consciously try to confirm these faulty beliefs. Some of the more common ineffective beliefs of difficult students are as follows:

- I am not capable.

- I am not worthwhile.

- I can't contribute in meaningful ways.

- I don't care.

- If I cannot be good at being good, I'll be good at being bad.

- Adults cannot be trusted.

- Adults do not like me.

- Adults never listen to me.

- It is better to get negative attention than to be ignored all together.

- I must hide the fact that I am afraid, weak, a poor reader, hurt, depressed, and so on.

- I must hurt others before they hurt me.

- It is better to be considered smart and lazy than to take a risk and be found to be dumb.

Difficult students may develop these ineffective beliefs from histories of unmet or frustrated basic needs, inconsistent discipline, overly harsh discipline, poor attachments or relationships with significant adults, failure, poor modeling, and personal or familial mental illness. When we realize this, we are better able to respond to the misbehavior and not take student behavior personally. It is most effective for the teacher not only to be aware of these ineffective beliefs but also to respond in ways that challenge them.

CHALLENGING INEFFECTIVE BELIEFS

Adults are wise to react in a way that does not confirm the beliefs but challenges them. Difficult students obtain a false sense of power when others confirm the faulty beliefs they hold about themselves. Effective strategies to challenge ineffective beliefs are responding unexpectedly, teaching students the ABCDE model of how thoughts influence behavior and emotions, and teaching students to self-evaluate and dispute ineffective beliefs.

Responding Unexpectedly

One of the best ways to challenge the beliefs of difficult students is to respond in an unexpected manner to their behavior. At first this may seem like a contradiction since difficult students need a high degree of structure. They do need structure, clear expectations for behavior, and the knowledge that consequences will be used; however, they do not need typical responses to their misbehavior. Difficult students are accustomed to a certain response from adults when they misbehave. Glasser (2000) concurs, stating, "A favorite trick of resistant students is to keep disrupting your teaching until you start to threaten or punish. When you do, they have gotten control of you and can now blame everything they're doing on you" (p. 25). Their perceptions are challenged when an adult does not respond in a predictable fashion. For example, responding with humor when the student expects wrath or responding with conversation and concern when the student expects punishment challenges the student's perceptions of that adult.

The ABCDE Model

Teachers can help students understand the power of their thoughts and beliefs by teaching them the ABCDE model (Ellis & Dryden, 1987), which helps children and adults understand the relationship between thoughts, behaviors, and emotions.

To help the reader conceptualize this model I use the example of a student who has just received a poor grade on a social studies test. In this model *A* stands for antecedent and refers to any real-world event. In my example, the real-world event would be the student receiving a low test grade. The *B* stands for beliefs and refers to thoughts that might occur after the event. For example, after receiving the low test grade, the student might have the following thoughts: "I always fail my tests; I hate social studies; I'm going to fail this class; this is horrible." The *C* stands for consequences and refers to the emotions and behaviors that will follow beliefs. In my example, these might be feelings of anger, helplessness, and anxiety or behaviors of quitting, crying, or acting out.

The most critical aspect of this model is that the real-world event (*A*) doesn't cause the emotion or behavior (*C*). The interpretations, beliefs, and thoughts (*B*) about the event lead to the emotions and behaviors. In other words, events in and of themselves do not cause emotions and behaviors. It is one's thoughts about these events that cause one's emotional and behavior response. In the example, some would incorrectly attribute the helpless behavior and angry emotion to the low test grade, but in reality it was the student's thoughts about the test grade that led to the emotion and behavior. It may help to further conceptualize this idea by thinking how the same event (low test grade) can precipitate a very different behavioral and emotional response from two different people. If the event in itself caused the emotions and behavior, then all people would have the same response to the same event. The *D* stands for disputing, and the *E* stands for effective beliefs. They are discussed in the next section.

Self-Evaluating and Disputing Ineffective Beliefs

Teachers can challenge ineffective beliefs by helping students self-evaluate the effectiveness of their thoughts. When students describe what they are experiencing with ineffective beliefs, we should help them self-evaluate the effectiveness of holding that belief by asking the following questions:

- What is the evidence for the thought?

- Does it help you to think about things in that way?

- Is there another way to look at the situation?

- Even if the thought is true, is it as bad as it seems?

These questions can be reworded for younger students and framed to make the children think like detectives looking for evidence. Returning to the previous example, we could ask the student what evidence exists that he or she always fails social studies tests and ask if it is really as horrible as it seems. After disputing, students are guided to develop more effective (E) or logical beliefs. For example, "I do better on my tests when I study" or "I'd probably like social studies better if I tried harder" or "I still have plenty of time to pull my grade up, and besides I did a good job on my project." Ineffective beliefs are usually stated with exaggerated, overgeneralized, polarized, or absolutistic words, such as *always, never, must, should,* and *have to.* It is helpful to train ourselves and our students to be on alert for these exaggerated and absolutistic words. Effective beliefs tend to be more flexible, logical, temporary, and specific to the situation. It may be helpful for the reader to go back and review the common ineffective beliefs of difficult students listed in the previous section. Do these beliefs reflect exaggerated, extreme, inflexible, or polarized thinking?

Benefits and Limitations of the ABCDE Model

One benefit of this model is that it is useful for both adults and children. All of us have a tendency to have ineffective thoughts and faulty logic. If you are feeling extremes in emotion, overly stressed, easily frustrated, agitated, angry, anxious, or depressed, faulty or ineffective beliefs are usually involved. In both children and adults, extreme emotions or behavior are usually the result of extreme beliefs.

One limitation of the ABCDE model is that students sometimes do not communicate their thoughts, which makes it difficult to help students dispute. Sometimes students will share their thoughts in journals, and all students are more likely to share their thoughts when they trust the person. When students exhibit extremes in emotion or behavior, we can usually assume that extreme beliefs are involved. We can ask students to discuss their thoughts by asking, "What thoughts were going through your head right before you got angry?"

Many difficult students believe that their teachers or any adult really can be trusted or cares for them. Unlike most other discipline programs, improving the teacher-student relationship is the primary intervention of choice with difficult students. The relationship-building strategies discussed in the following section serve to challenge the beliefs of these students by providing new and unexpected interaction patterns. Although many times difficult students are the hardest children to establish a positive relationship with, they are most certainly the ones who need it the most.

RELATIONSHIP-BUILDING PLAN FOR DIFFICULT STUDENTS

Research tells us that teachers respond to and treat difficult students differently than they treat typical students (Brophy & Good, 2000). Teachers give difficult students less wait time, praise, interaction, and positive attention but give them more criticism. This finding does not bode well for difficult students since these students need extra positive support and overt knowledge that the teacher cares for them and believes they can succeed. Teachers are usually not aware of their differential treatment of difficult students. We need to develop plans to avoid these interaction pitfalls and to ensure the priority of a positive teacher-student relationship.

Imagine the number and degree of negative adult interactions that difficult students experience in a typical day. The simplest plan for decreasing the number of negative interactions is to ask the difficult student one nonacademic question per day. Some other teachers make it a point to have a positive word or greeting the day after having to address a student about his or her behavior. Other plans may involve noticing and commenting on positive behaviors more frequently than negative behaviors. This strategy is very effective at changing the nature of interactions with difficult students.

The more difficult the student, the more important it is to use positive and relationship-building strategies over punitive ones. These students need to know they are needed, wanted, and can contribute to the class, and they require a relationship of unconditional acceptance, consistency, and trust (Pianta, 1999). As Mendler (2000) states, "We must make it as hard as possible for students to reject their education" (p. 48). These students are often difficult to bond with because of their background and disposition, and they usually do not go out of their way to interact with teachers. Therefore, connecting with these students involves skill, time, and patience, and it requires thinking outside the box and doing the unexpected. Three strategies for bonding with difficult students, which I discuss in the following sections, are nondirectional dialogue, input seeking, and a 4 to 1 ratio plan.

Nondirectional Dialogue

The goal in nondirectional dialogue is to make an effort to talk with students about anything other than the behaviors or problems present in the classroom. It is considered nondirectional because the adult does not tell the students what they need to be doing or discuss past problems with them. I have already discussed the importance of effective feedback, recognition, and praise, but this technique is simpler: it only involves paying attention to students, regardless of their behavior. This communication can take place during class, between classes, during free time, at lunch, or during transitions. This strategy is similar to another strategy referred to as banking time, which holds that if enough positive relationship bonding has accrued (deposits), then the relationship can withstand stress or conflict (withdrawals).

Similarly, Fay and Funk (1995) advocate for teachers to provide students with as many opportunities to make choices as possible. Every choice that teachers give students is in a sense an investment or deposit. Students who build these choice deposits are willing to comply when the teacher needs to take a withdrawal, which occurs in times when choices are not possible or reasonable. Teachers have been able to gain compliance from difficult students by saying, "I have given you many choices, but now I really need for you to . . . " This strategy communicates to the student that he or she is unconditionally accepted and important.

The critical component to remember is that banking time and nondirectional dialogue are not contingent on the child's behavior; in other words, the student does not have to earn it. If students had to earn these relationship builders, the ones who needed them the most would be the least likely to earn them. Another key component is that by not discussing and focusing on the problems in the classroom, you are responding paradoxically or unexpectedly. Most of the interactions that these youngsters have with adults involve coercion to change and reminders about their shortcomings. Although teachers do this with good intentions, it often backfires: It can communicate that they are important only if they get good grades, do homework, or comply. Another strategy with a similar goal is the 2-minute intervention (Mendler, 2000). In this method the teacher spends 2 uninterrupted minutes, for 10 consecutive days, building the relationship with the student but, again, avoiding any discussion of classroom problems.

Think about your interactions with difficult students. Are they directed at changing the student or showing personal interest in them? Are the interactions conditional or unconditional? How do these interactions challenge or confirm the beliefs that adults don't like them, don't listen to them, and can't be trusted?

Input Seeking

Seeking student input about the class makes the student feel valued and important and gives them a positive voice. In a simple way, this strategy helps to challenge their belief that adults never listen to them and assists in meeting their unmet power and freedom needs. In addition, since most difficult students have never been asked to give input about the class, this strategy challenges their beliefs by doing the unexpected.

The teacher might ask the student about what he or she likes or dislikes about the class and what the teacher could do to make the class better. This is often very difficult for teachers since it requires relinquishing control and opening themselves up for criticism. The teacher does not need to accommodate all the wishes of the student—making even a small change in your class based on the input will give the student much positive power and ownership, which reduces the chances that the student will attempt to gain negative power by disturbing the class or undermining the teacher.

After the teacher has made a change based on the student's input, the teacher can use negotiation to get some of what he or she would like from the student. For example, the teacher may say, "I'd be willing to continue to lecture less if you would be willing to do some homework" or "I'd be willing to accept a report on another subject that you are more interested in if you would be willing to raise your hand before speaking." The extreme opposite of this approach is the my-way-or-the-highway approach, which sends the message to the student that he or she must change, or else. Remember, difficult students are accustomed to this approach and have received this message numerous times in the past, so they are not likely to respond to it.

4 to 1 Ratio Plan

This strategy leads to more positive overall interactions between the teacher and student. For many difficult students, negative attention is better than no attention. This strategy helps to prevent the student's negative attention seeking. In this strategy the teacher actually monitors the number of negative and positive interactions that occur with the targeted student. The determining factor on whether or not an interaction is positive or negative is what the student is doing at the time of the interaction (Sprick et al., 1998). A negative interaction is counted each time the teacher must give a consequence or talk to the student about misbehavior. A positive interaction is any interaction that occurs when the student is following the rules. The goal is to interact with the student about four times more frequently when he or she is behaving appropriately versus when the student is not behaving appropriately. This is a difficult but powerful strategy.

It is important to keep track of actual numbers, especially at first. One way to track your interactions is to place four paper clips in your pocket each time a negative interaction occurs. The paper clips serve as reminders that you owe the student four positive interactions. Each time you interact with the student when they are behaving, remove one clip from your pocket. It is not necessary that the four interactions consist of you praising the student for behaving appropriately. The only rule is that the interactions not be corrective or negative.

When we strengthen our relationships with our difficult students, we challenge their ineffective beliefs about significant adults. The best interventions, when used without building a positive teacher-student relationship, are of little long-term value. Next, I discuss using a team approach to develop a behavior support plan.

DEVELOPING BEHAVIOR SUPPORT PLANS

Some students with chronic or severe behavior problems require a behavior support plan. Behavior support plans or behavior intervention plans are usually developed collaboratively by a team of teachers, support staff, and parents, who ideally are trained in functional assessment and behavior plans. Developing these plans is part of a philosophy and methodology called positive behavior supports. The purpose of this section is to help the classroom teacher understand the purpose, philosophy, and terminology involved in behavior support planning, so he or she may begin to play a more integral role in the development of behavior support plans for students.

The purpose of a behavior support plan is to gain a thorough understanding of the student's behavior and its possible motives, so the student can be taught more effective ways of satisfying his or her needs. In other words, how do we support this particular student to learn more effective behaviors? Support can come from skill building (e.g., social skills training, anger management), environmental changes (e.g., altering triggers or events that may precipitate misbehavior), and teaching adaptations (e.g., curriculum changes, increasing support and feedback). These plans are not designed to focus on reactive strategies and consequences because these methods have likely already been unsuccessful.

Functional assessments determine the motive or function of the behavior and usually involve collecting multiple types of information, such as school records; developmental history; parent, student, and teacher interviews; student strengths, weaknesses, and interests; medical and psychiatric history; observations in multiple settings; baseline data of severity, frequency, and intensity of behavior; and responses to past interventions. A thorough functional assessment usually finds answers to four critical questions:

1. *In what circumstance is the behavior most likely to occur?* Does the behavior occur or vary with certain peers, instructional formats, academic subjects, time of day, or under different sensory exposures?

2. *In what circumstance is the behavior least likely to occur?* Are there some people, times of the day, or classes where the behavior occurs less frequently or is absent?

3. *What does the student obtain from displaying the behavior?* Does the student obtain social status, stimulation, adult attention, and more assistance from displaying the behavior?

4. *What does the student escape from by displaying the behavior?* Does the student avoid academic tasks, frustration, unwanted social interaction, loud noises, or crowded classrooms by displaying the behavior?

A thorough functional assessment should lead to a valid hypothesis of motive for the behavior and a more effective way for the student to satisfy the need or motivation. The assessment could also suggest a method to alter the learning environment, so the student no longer has the motivation or need. The assessment should provide a goal statement and the specific skills the student will need to accomplish the goal. For example, a goal would be for a student to ask for assistance when frustrated instead of swearing. The skills needed in this example would be to recognize cues to frustration and verbal practice in seeking assistance. If the team determines that the behavior occurs when academic work is at the student's frustration level rather than at the student's instructional level, then an environmental or learning adaptation would be suggested.

The behavior intervention plan is driven by the functional assessment or collection of behavioral data and background information. The success of the behavior support plan hinges on the accuracy and thoroughness of the functional assessment. According to Wright (1999) behavior support plans should address how the current environment supports or prevents problem behavior; the purpose of the behavior for the student; possible reasons why the behavior continues; necessary environmental, instructional, and curriculum adaptations; and how replacement behaviors will be taught. Last, effective behavior support plans should describe the roles and responsibilities of all involved, a person to monitor intervention integrity (whether the plan is followed as agreed on), steps or scripts to follow if the behavior occurs, parental consent, and dates to review progress.

One final note on behavior support plans. The federal Individuals With Disabilities Education Act states that when a student's behavior impedes his or her learning or that of others, the Individual Education Plan team needs to address these behaviors with positive behavioral interventions, strategies, and supports, a procedure explicitly called for in cases where a student with a disability is suspended for more than 10 school days. This means that classroom teachers will increasingly be called on to assist in the development and the implementation of behavior support plans. The reader who is interested in more information on behavior support planning is directed to the Web site for Positive Behavioral Interventions and Supports (http://www.pbis.org).

SUMMARY OF MAIN POINTS

- We make three critical errors in dealing with difficult students: overreliance on punishment, targeting too many behaviors for change, and failing to look for exceptions to the problems.

- Difficult students have ineffective beliefs that influence their emotions and behaviors.

- Teachers can challenge these ineffective beliefs by responding unexpectedly, teaching students the ABCDE model, assisting them in disputing ineffective beliefs, and strengthening the teacher-student relationship.

- Relationship-building strategies of nondirectional dialogue, input seeking, and 4 to 1 ratio plans can change the interactional patterns and beliefs that difficult students have about themselves and significant adults at school.

- Behavior support planning involves developing a hypothesis about the needs and motivations of student behavior and teaching the student more effective replacement behaviors that address the same needs and motivations.

QUESTIONS FOR DISCUSSION AND SELF-EVALUATION

1. What are some other ineffective beliefs that your students have?

2. How can the ABCDE model assist you as a teacher in managing your own emotions and behaviors?

3. Can you give an example of an exception to the problem for a current or former difficult student you had? How could you build on this exception or strength?

4. What are some strategies that you are already using that are effective with difficult students?

5. What is the ratio of positive to negative interactions in your classroom? Why is this important?

ACTION PLAN

As a result of something that I learned in this chapter I plan to (be specific in your answer):

_____

_____

_____

RECOMMENDED RESOURCES

Center for Effective Collaboration and Practice. (1998). *Addressing student problem behavior—An IEP team's introduction to functional behavioral assessment and behavior intervention plans* (2nd ed.). Washington, DC: Federal Resource Center for Special Education. This book is designed more for special educators but provides an excellent introduction to functional assessment and positive behavior support planning.

Curwin, R., & Mendler, A. (1999b). *Discipline with dignity for challenging youth.* Bloomington, IN: National Educational Service. This book provides excellent strategies for changing teacher attitudes and beliefs about difficult students and choosing effective discipline strategies. It also contains ideas for specific populations and special discipline problems.

Koegel, L. K., Koegel, R. L., & Dunlap, G. (1996). *Positive behavioral support: Including people with difficult behavior in the community.* Baltimore: Paul H. Brookes. This books uses a variety of expert authors for an in-depth look at positive behavioral support planning. Classroom teachers, especially those with students with behavior disorders, can benefit from the section on education issues.

Kottler, J. (2002). *Students who drive you crazy: Succeeding with resistant, unmotivated, and otherwise difficult young people.* Thousand Oaks, CA: Corwin. The author takes an interesting look at how teachers view different behaviors differently and what teachers can do to change their own behavior and their students' behavior. There is also a chapter on dealing with difficult parents and colleagues.

Mendler, A. (2000). *Motivating students who don't care.* Bloomington, IN: National Educational Service. This book provides numerous strategies that address student motivation problems and stresses how positive relationships increase motivation.

Chapter Ten

Reflecting on Your Classroom Management Skills

"I have noticed that happy people are constantly evaluating themselves, and unhappy people are constantly evaluating others."

—Glasser (1996)

CHAPTER OBJECTIVES

In this chapter the reader will learn:

- School and classroom barriers to a relationship-driven approach
- The central tenets of the relationship-driven classroom
- Tools to assess a relationship-driven classroom

BARRIERS TO A RELATIONSHIP-DRIVEN APPROACH

There are many barriers that we most overcome to make relationships a priority in our schools and classrooms. This book grew out of my personal involvement in developing a violence prevention program. I realized that preserving and enhancing relationships and classroom management were being neglected in many prevention programs. Despite a solid and growing research base stating the importance of relationships, they were not a priority.

In the next section the barriers to a relationship-driven classroom are addressed. The barriers diminish both the student's connection to school and his or her relationship to a significant adult at school. I understand that alone the classroom teacher may have little influence on some of these factors since they are entrenched in school systems. Many of the barriers are school-wide, systemic, and philosophical factors that impede a relationship-driven approach. In outlining the barriers, I mean to begin a dialogue about the importance of relationships and eliminating policies that interfere with their development.

Prevention Incompatibility

Many effective school improvement and violence prevention programs are being undermined by classroom management and school discipline practices that are incompatible or, at best, poor models for these programs. For example, conflict management and peer mediation programs are increasing in an effort to prevent violence. If a school is implementing a conflict management program that strives for peaceful resolution of conflicts through win-win solutions, but the staff is using classroom management techniques that escalate conflict or result in win-lose solutions, most if not all of the benefits are lost. We need discipline strategies that are compatible with and complement these worthwhile school improvement and prevention programs.

Overreliance on Punishment and Suspensions

Many discipline strategies are punishment oriented, especially those used with difficult students. These students, who most need relationship building and positive connections to school, are the ones who receive them the least. Schools and communities look to harsher punishments and push-out strategies, such as suspensions and expulsion, to prevent violence. It is ironic that we remove from school those students who have the greatest need to be positively connected to school and teachers. These strategies send the unwanted message that we push out our problems instead of solving them.

While I do believe that students need to be removed from school for safety reasons, research has shown that the majority of these suspensions are for nondangerous behaviors, such as disruptiveness, defiance, and truancy (Skiba & Peterson, 1999). Suspensions are overused with minorities, lower income students, and disabled students and are related to increased dropout rates (Skiba & Peterson, 1999). In addition, cumulative discipline policies that assign more severe punishments each time the student gets into trouble are not effective and serve to further alienate these students from school.

When schools rely on punitive strategies, they may be failing to address critical school climate issues that contribute to student misbehavior, alienation, and violence. In most of the 37 school shootings described in the federal report *An Interim Report on the Prevention of Targeted School Violence in Schools* the attackers listed revenge as a primary motive in the attack, and many of the school shooters reported being victims of harassment and bullying (U.S. Secret Service Safe School Initiative, 2000). We need new tools, rather than more stringent and more frequent punishments, to make our schools safe. We need to use strategies that preserve relationships and teach students new and more effective skills.

Ignoring Interactive Systems

It has been my experience that schools focus behavioral and academic interventions on changing the student, which neglects other possible factors that contribute to student behavior, such as school and classroom climate, effective classroom management, teacher-student relationships, peer relationships, and effective instruction and curriculum. Students, in comparison to teachers, have less maturity, self-regulation, and general resources at their disposal for change. Certainly students should assume some responsibility for change; however, we tend to put the majority of responsibility for change on the student. Student behavior problems do not arise solely in isolation but are created or exist in the context of relationships and environments. This explains why students exhibit different problems in different environments and may actually have no problems with certain teachers and subjects. We must be willing to take an honest look at all factors (including ourselves) that influence behavior in school.

The Assumption of Behavioral Skill

We must take heed of the dangerous assumption that students know or should know how, when, and why to behave appropriately. They may lack this knowledge or lack self-control. We do know that when students are told what behaviors are expected of them in advance and allowed to practice them prior to an activity or transition, they are more likely to display appropriate behavior. We need to treat behavioral deficits much like we do academic deficits. If a student is struggling with mathematics facts, we assume that remediation is necessary, or if a student is struggling with staying in his or her seat or is disrupting class, we assume that the student knows fully how to act but is deciding not to. We need to give behavior the same educational benefit of the doubt that we give academics.

Overemphasis on Technical Teaching Skills

Administrators can place too much emphasis on technical teaching skills. Evaluations of both teachers on staff and potential employees often put too much emphasis on technical skills (e.g., a good demonstration lesson) and not enough emphasis on the ability of the teacher to establish and maintain relationships, build rapport, and model social-emotional competence. In most states, to be hired as a firefighter you must go through rigorous physical and psychological testing. Do we value psychological or social-emotional competence in firefighters more so than in teachers?

Effective technical teaching skills are much less powerful when positive and personal relational factors are absent. In this regard, education and teaching are similar to the field of counseling. In education, as in the field of counseling, the techniques or theoretical orientation of the teacher, helper, or therapist are not as important as the quality of the relationship between client and helper (Lambert, 1992). If positive and personal relationships are going to be a priority for teachers, administrators must also place high value on these teaching components.

THE CENTRAL TENETS
OF RELATIONSHIP-DRIVEN
CLASSROOM MANAGEMENT

In this section the central tenets of a relationship-driven classroom are highlighted along with the chapter or chapters where the tenet is explained in the book. The central tenets are presented here to help the reader better conceptualize the main themes of the relationship-driven approach, which are interwoven throughout the book:

1. A proactive classroom strives to prevent misbehavior from occurring by discussing, teaching, monitoring, and practicing the classroom expectations and rules. Another goal is to strive to satisfy students' basic needs for belonging, power, freedom, and fun so that the motivation to get these needs met in a negative or ineffective manner diminishes. In addition, a proactive classroom strives to establish a classroom climate characterized by positive and personal relationships, emotional safety, trust, mutual respect, and cooperation. (Chapter 3)

2. Positive teacher-student relationships do the following:
- Increase academic achievement and motivation
- Decrease risk-taking behaviors, such as drug use, dropout, aggressiveness, and violence
- Increase coping skills and resilience
- Enhance peer relationships (Chapter 4)

3. Relationship-driven teachers use self-evaluation often in the classroom. They self-evaluate the effectiveness of their relational and discipline practices, and they encourage students to self-evaluate the effectiveness of their behavior and work. Self-evaluation can enhance self-awareness, self-control, ownership, responsibility, and pride. (Chapters 2 and 7)

4. Punishment is any consequence that involves pain, hurt, or loss. While experiencing pain, hurt, and loss is a part of life, one does not have to experience these feelings to change behavior. Punishment hurts relationships and fails to teach responsibility and internal control. In fact, punishment may hinder the development of responsibility since the student often focuses his or her energies on the punishment, the punisher, and the associated negative feelings. (Chapters 2 and 7)

5. The very same social-emotional skills that are important in preventing misbehavior are also prerequisites to effective learning. Self-control, problem solving, social skills, self-efficacy, and optimism can enhance learning, behavior, quality of life, and resilience. If we neglect any of these components, we fail to tap in to the full learning potential of the individual. The relationship-driven classroom teacher views these social-emotional factors as complements not competitors to reaching academic achievement and behavioral goals. (Chapter 5)

6. Relationship-driven teachers honor diversity and model tolerance, not only in religion, race, creed, and color, but also especially in cognitive/academic diversity. They use effective instructional strategies that increase achievement and motivation and reduce misbehavior. In addition they use instructional adaptations to maximize the success of diverse learners, and they have a deep understanding of the interrelationship between academic success and behavior. (Chapter 6)

7. The teacher regularly uses the following seven questions to self-assess the consequences used in the classroom:
- Does it bring me closer to the student?
- Would it encourage me to change my own behavior?
- Does it model the social-emotional skills that I want my students to possess?
- Does it instruct or teach a more appropriate behavior?
- Does it interfere with the flow of the lesson?
- Does it allow the learner a choice to redirect and receive instruction?
- Is it effective? (Chapter 8)

8. Behaviors are complex and multidetermined. Behaviors can result from the interaction or relationship between teacher and student or student and the instructional environment. Interventions need to address all factors that influence student behavior, such as social or behavioral skill deficits, environmental and learning conditions, and poor teacher-student interactions. Interventions that focus only on changing the student reveal a limited understanding of the interactional nature of behavior and are doomed to fail. (Chapter 8)

9. Difficult students have many ineffective beliefs that influence their emotions and behaviors. Teachers can challenge these

ineffective beliefs by responding unexpectedly, by teaching them how to dispute their ineffective beliefs, and by strengthening the teacher-student relationship. Punitive techniques increase distance between the teacher and student and confirm the negative beliefs of the student. (Chapter 9)

TOOLS FOR ASSESSING THE LEARNING ENVIRONMENT

I have developed two scales to assist educators in evaluating the presence of the key components of the relationship-driven classroom. The first, a teacher assessment consisting of 25 questions related to the classroom, is called the Relationship-Driven Classroom Assessment Scale (Teacher Form). The second, the Relationship-Driven Classroom Assessment Scale (Student Form), requires the students to answer 23 questions about his or her perceptions of the classroom.

Students will need some guidance and reassurance from you prior to completing their scale. They will need to be reassured of unanimity and the purpose of the assessment—to make the class more effective. The students most likely have never had a teacher inquire about their perceptions of the class. If the teacher shares the results with the students in a nondefensive manner, and more important, makes changes based on student input, it will send the message to the students that they are important and have ownership and responsibility in the way the class operates. The importance of giving students a voice cannot be overemphasized because it is related to the basic needs of power and freedom discussed in Chapter 3.

The statements on both scales are based on the key characteristics of the relationship-driven classroom discussed throughout the book. The reader will notice letters followed by a number in parentheses following each statement. These represent the chapter in which this concept is discussed in the book. For example, the first item on the teacher form is *I regularly use relationship builders (listening, supporting, encouraging, negotiation, befriending, caring, welcoming, personal/nonacademic dialogue) in my interactions with all students* **(RD4).** In this example, **RD** stands for the category of relationship-driven and **4** stands for Chapter 4. A key is provided at the end of each scale. If one or more questions are answered negatively in each category, the reader can go back to the section in the chapter to get ideas for improvement. If the reader would like even more information, he or she is directed to the recommended resources at the end of that chapter.

The reader should note that the following scales are not empirically validated or researched. They are intended to assist in teacher self-evaluation based on the ideas in this book. The reader who is interested in an empirically validated and researched evaluation tool for the classroom is referred to The Instructional Environment System or TIES-II (Ysseldyke & Christenson, 1993), which provides a more thorough and research-validated tool for classroom evaluation. This instrument assesses 12 instructional factors that are critical to effective teaching: instructional presentation, classroom environment, teacher expectations, cognitive emphasis, motivational strategies, relevant practice, academic engaged time, informed feedback, adaptive instruction, progress evaluation, instructional planning, and student understanding.

RELATIONSHIP-DRIVEN CLASSROOM ASSESSMENT SCALE (TEACHER FORM)

Read each statement below, self-evaluate, and circle your answer.

1. I regularly use the relationship builders (listening, supporting, encouraging, negotiating, befriending, caring, welcoming, personal/nonacademic dialogue) in my interactions with all students. **(RD4)**

Most of the time   **Sometimes**   **Never**

2. I have eliminated or reduced the use of relationship barriers (blaming, assuming, threatening, punishing, yelling, shaming) in my interactions with students. **(RD4)**

Most of the time   **Sometimes**   **Never**

3. I strive to find a balance between firmness, fairness, and friendliness in my interactions with students and the entire class. **(RD4)**

Most of the time   **Sometimes**   **Never**

4. I am consistent in that I make sure students know what is expected, monitor behavior and compliance, and provide feedback or consequences as necessary. **(RD4)**

Most of the time   **Sometimes**   **Never**

5. I am consistent in that I avoid giving too many reminders, chances, or ultimatums for student compliance. **(RD4)**

Most of the time   **Sometimes**   **Never**

6. I communicate to my students that mistakes are a natural part of learning and are opportunities to improve learning. **(PRO3)**

Most of the time   **Sometimes**   **Never**

7. I have reduced or eliminated threat from my interactions with my students. **(PRO3)**

Most of the time   **Sometimes**   **Never**

8. I make efforts to encourage students by using effective praise characterized by being specific and genuine, recognizing effort more than ability, and not comparing performance to others. **(PRO3)**

Most of the time　　　　　**Sometimes**　　　　　**Never**

9. I teach and allow students to practice classroom procedures prior to activities and transitions. **(PRO3)**

Most of the time　　　　　**Sometimes**　　　　　**Never**

10. I acknowledge and recognize positive student behavior much more than I acknowledge negative behavior. **(PRO3)**

Most of the time　　　　　**Sometimes**　　　　　**Never**

11. I use effective instructional techniques, such as setting clear goals, encouraging students to set personalized learning goals, increasing active student involvement, and providing immediate, specific, and frequent feedback. **(EAI6)**

Most of the time　　　　　**Sometimes**　　　　　**Never**

12. I use strategies to increase student motivation, such as increasing task value and students' expectancy of success, helping students make connections between effort and success, and allowing student choices about learning. **(EAI6)**

Most of the time　　　　　**Sometimes**　　　　　**Never**

13. I honor all types of diversity but especially cognitive or academic skill diversity in my students by adapting instruction to meet a variety of learning needs. **(EAI6)**

Most of the time　　　**Sometimes**　　　　　　**Never**

14. My responses to student misbehavior are more instructional than punitive (i.e., teach what and how to do the behavior rather than simply telling what not to do). **(EC8)**

Most of the time　　　　　**Sometimes**　　　　　**Never**

15. If a student is not acting responsibly, I assume that the student needs to be taught the skill or subskill of responsibility. **(RO7)**

Most of the time   **Sometimes**   **Never**

16. I build student responsibility by encouraging students to self-evaluate and develop a plan for more effective behavior rather than focusing on obedience. **(RO7)**

Most of the time   **Sometimes**   **Never**

17. I do not take student behavior personally when disciplining students since it is the student's best attempt at meeting his or her needs at that time. **(PRO3)**

Most of the time   **Sometimes**   **Never**

18. In my classroom, students have many positive opportunities to satisfy their basic needs for belonging (acceptance), power (competence), freedom (choices), fun, and security. **(PRO3)**

Most of the time   **Sometimes**   **Never**

19. I strive to build student resilience by creating caring relationships, maintaining high expectations with necessary supports, and providing opportunities for meaningful contribution and involvement. **(RES1)**

Most of the time   **Sometimes**   **Never**

20. I maintain a positive and enthusiastic attitude by managing stress effectively, exercising, and practicing the skills of optimism. **(TA2)**

Most of the time   **Sometimes**   **Never**

21. I set high and realistic expectations for my students. **(TA2)**

Most of the time   **Sometimes**   **Never**

22. I use consequences that preserve the teacher-student relationship, do not interrupt the flow of the lesson, model social-emotional skills, allow for choice, teach or instruct a more

effective behavior, and reflect how I would like to be treated after a mistake. **(EC8)**

Most of the time　　　　　**Sometimes**　　　　　**Never**

23. I strive to use consequences that build self-control rather than obedience. **(EC8)**

Most of the time　　　　　**Sometimes**　　　　　**Never**

24. I am aware of the ineffective beliefs that difficult students have, and I strive to challenge them by responding unexpectedly, by helping them learn to dispute these beliefs, and by incorporating relationship-building strategies. **(DS9)**

Most of the time　　　　　**Sometimes**　　　　　**Never**

25. I model and teach important social-emotional skills that build resilience, reduce misbehavior, and increase achievement, such as social skills, self-control, problem solving, self-efficacy, and optimism. **(SES5)**

Most of the time　　　　　**Sometimes**　　　　　**Never**

Category Key: RES = Resilience; TA = Teacher Attributes; PRO = Proactive; RD = Relationship-Driven; SES = Social-Emotional Skills; EAI = Effective Adaptive Instruction; RO = Responsibility-Oriented; EC = Effective Consequences; DS = Difficult Students

*If one or more statements in each category are answered negatively refer, to the chapter for specific suggestions.

RELATIONSHIP-DRIVEN CLASSROOM ASSESSMENT SCALE (STUDENT FORM)

Please read the statements below and circle one answer. If your teacher does a very good job, circle **Most of the time.** If your teacher does an average job, circle **Sometimes.** If your teacher does a poor job, circle **Never** and explain why. Your honesty will make this a better class and will make your teacher a better teacher.

1. My teacher treats all students in a friendly and fair manner. **(RD4)**

Most of the time　　　　　**Sometimes**　　　　　**Never**

　　If **Never,** please explain.

_____

_____

_____

2.　　My teacher is very clear about what behavior is expected in different situations. **(PRO3)**

Most of the time　　　　　**Sometimes**　　　　　**Never**

　　If **Never,** please explain.

_____

_____

_____

3.　　My teacher gives all students opportunities to be involved in helping the classroom, school, and community. **(RES1)**

Most of the time　　　　　**Sometimes**　　　　　**Never**

　　If **Never,** please explain.

_____

_____

_____

4.   My teacher almost never belittles, lectures, nags, or embarrasses me. **(RD4)**

Most of the time   **Sometimes**   **Never**

If **Never,** please explain.

_____

_____

_____

5.   I feel safe in this classroom from threats, ridicule, yelling, and anger, from both the teacher and the other students. **(RD4)**

Most of the time   **Sometimes**   **Never**

If **Never,** please explain.

_____

_____

_____

6.   My teacher is patient, calm, and does not get easily upset and stressed. **(TA2)**

Most of the time   **Sometimes**   **Never**

If **Never,** please explain.

_____

_____

_____

7.   My teacher returns papers and tests quickly, teaches us why certain answers are right and wrong, and expects us to correct our mistakes. **(EAI6)**

Most of the time   **Sometimes**   **Never** ·

If **Never,** please explain.

_____

_____

_____

8.   My teacher tells us what we are going to learn about and asks us to set personal goals about what we want to learn about the topic. **(EAI6)**

Most of the time   **Sometimes**   **Never**

If **Never,** please explain.

_____

_____

_____

9.   My teacher acts like he or she expects me to act. **(SES5)**

Most of the time   **Sometimes**   **Never**

If **Never**, please explain.

_____

_____

_____

10.   My teacher lets me make some choices about this class and my own learning. **(EAI6)**

Most of the time   **Sometimes**   **Never**

If **Never,** please explain.

_____

_____

_____

11.   When a student misbehaves, the teacher tries to teach a more effective behavior instead of just punishing the student. **(EC8)**

Most of the time   **Sometimes**   **Never**

If **Never,** please explain.

_____

_____

_____

12.   My teacher frequently checks to see if rules and expectations are being followed and gives us consequences when they are not. **(RD4)**

Most of the time   **Sometimes**   **Never**

If **Never,** please explain.

_____

_____

_____

13.   My teacher treats all students equally well (no students are favored over others). **(RD4)**

Most of the time   **Sometimes**   **Never**

If **Never,** please explain.

_____

_____

_____

14.   My teacher encourages and challenges me to be the best student possible and gives me support when I need it. **(TA2)**

Most of the time   **Sometimes**   **Never**

If **Never,** please explain.

_____

_____

_____

15.   My teacher believes I am capable of doing quality work. **(TA2)**

Most of the time   · **Sometimes**   **Never**

If **Never,** please explain.

_____

_____

_____

16.   My teacher really likes the subject or subjects he or she teaches. **(TA2)**

Most of the time   **Sometimes**   **Never**

If **Never,** please explain.

_____

_____

_____

17.   My teacher expects us to make plans to solve problems that arise in the classroom. **(RO7)**

Most of the time   **Sometimes**   **Never**

If **Never,** please explain.

_____

_____

_____

18.   My teacher gives us compliments and recognizes when we do something good more than when we do something bad. **(PRO3)**

Most of the time   **Sometimes**   **Never**

If **Never,** please explain.

_____

_____

_____

19.   I feel accepted by the teacher and other students. **(PRO3)**

Most of the time   **Sometimes**   **Never**

If **Never,** please explain.

20.   I feel competent (able to be successful) in class. **(PRO3)**

Most of the time   **Sometimes**   **Never**

If **Never,** please explain.

_____

_____

_____

21.   Learning in this class is fun. **(PRO3)**

Most of the time   **Sometimes**   **Never**

If **Never,** please explain.

_____

_____

_____

22.   My teacher knows me personally, listens to me, is interested in me, and cares about me. **(RD4)**

Most of the time   **Sometimes**   **Never**

If **Never,** please explain.

_____

_____

_____

23.   I am not afraid to take risks, ask questions, and make mistakes in this class. **(PRO3)**

Most of the time   **Sometimes**   **Never**

If **Never,** please explain.

_____

_____

_____

Please write any other information on the back of this sheet that you feel will make this a better class or that will help you learn more.

For Teacher Use: Category Key: RES = Resilience; TA = Teacher Attributes; PRO = Proactive; RD = Relationship-Driven; SES = Social-Emotional Skills; EAI = Effective Adaptive Instruction; RO = Responsibility-Oriented; EC = Effective Consequences; DS = Difficult Students

Resource: Further Strategies for Adapting Instruction

The sections that follow provide the reader with some additional information on adapting instruction that was discussed in Chapter 6. The sections include general instructional approaches that accommodate diverse learners followed by specific classroom adaptations for presenting directions, note taking, organization, homework, testing, and grading.

INSTRUCTIONAL APPROACHES THAT ACCOMMODATE DIVERSE LEARNERS

The more these instructional practices are used with the entire class, the less the teacher will have to make adaptations for individual students (Deschenes et al., 1994).

- Cooperative learning
- Thematic, integrated approaches
- Multidimensional student grouping
- Short-term skill-based grouping
- Student presentations and projects
- Role-plays, skits, and plays

- Peer supports
- Authentic assessment
- Multimedia presentations
- Community-referenced projects
- Multiple intelligences (information is more likely to be recalled when it is stored in different areas of the brain)

ADAPTATIONS FOR NOTE TAKING

- Teach mind mapping or webbing—a visual graphic form in which information is distilled into key words and pictures.

- Teach students how to take notes. A teacher could tape-record the lesson and then take notes on an overhead while listening to the tape with the class.

- Teach students how to summarize and abbreviate.

- Allow a peer to make two sets of notes, using carbon paper or a copier.

- Provide time for note swapping or exchanges periodically.

- Allow use of a tape recorder.

- Allow use of a word processor.

ADAPTATIONS FOR ORGANIZATION

- Provide time during class or at end of class to organize materials.

- Assign a study buddy or peer to help with organization and have the peer and the student in need exchange phone numbers.

- Color-code books and notebooks.

- Place all materials in one binder.

- Encourage students to use one side of a notebook or folder for take home/leave home materials and the other side for take home/return papers.

- Allow for an extra set of books at home, if available.

- Place reminder checklists on desks or in lockers.

- Assign a locker helper.

- Have scheduled or unscheduled notebook checks to reward effective organization.

- Have periodic notebook clean-out times to sort and dump, using help from a peer, volunteer, or tutor.

ADAPTATIONS FOR PRESENTING DIRECTIONS

- Lower your voice or wait for the class to get quiet before giving directions.

- Use a signal or cue to gain attention prior to giving directions.

- Provide visual and verbal directions.

- Have individual students repeat directions to check for understanding.

- Avoid multistep directions, unless they are accompanied by written directions.

ADAPTATIONS FOR HOMEWORK

- Provide a written homework policy for parents.

- Use a homework assignment book, agenda mate, or log to write assignments, tests, and due dates.

- Monitor and adjust the quantity of homework.

- Reduce the quantity or number of problems.

- Avoid requiring students to copy questions and then write answers.

- For long-range projects, provide a finished model, teach process and time management, and break down tasks into smaller steps with deadlines.

- For long-range projects, use a project calendar.

- Assign study buddy with phone link.

- Allow students to start homework in class to avoid practicing the wrong process. Homework that is begun in class is more likely to be completed at home.

- Write down assignments in a routine location in the classroom.

- Write comments on homework papers for greater impact.

ADAPTATIONS FOR TESTING/GRADING

- Allow dictation or oral responses to test questions.

- Allow test to be read aloud to the student.

- Use open-book and open-note tests.

- Do not penalize for spelling and handwriting.

- Allow an alternate assignment in lieu of a test or as a replacement.

- Provide options for students to demonstrate knowledge, such as reviews, projects, interviews, maps, graphs, and extra homework.

- Allow students to list ideas instead of complete sentences.

- Allow extra time to complete or only grade what was finished.

- Create easier versions of test.

- Simplify terminology and reading level on tests.

- Allow test retakes and give ample credit for improvement. When the two grades are averaged, it can be discouraging.

- Use study guides that use the same format as does the test.

- Provide more time for review (quiz bowls, study buddy, etc.).

- Bonus points for parent signature stating the parent and student studied together.

- Score some students on priority items only, giving extra credit for answers beyond priority items.

- Eliminate one of the choices in a multiple choice exam, so students have fewer items to choose from and less reading to do.

- Give shorter tests covering less material more often. Avoid long exams.

- Grade student effort in addition to performance.

- Allow students to practice speculating on possible test questions or to develop test questions.

- Review test format after test is passed out. Highlight or underline important words or test directions.

- Grade on individual progress basis rather than on grade-level expectations.

References

Adams, M. (1990). *Beginning to read: Thinking and learning about print.* Cambridge, MA: MIT Press.

Algozzine, B., & Ysseldyke, J. (1997). *Strategies and tactics for effective instruction.* Longmont, CO: Sopris West.

Anderman, L., & Midgley, C. (1998). *Motivation and middle school students.* Champaign, IL: ERIC. (ERIC Document Reproduction Service No. ED421281)

Battistich, V., Solomon, D., Watson, M., & Schaps, E. (1997). Caring school communities. *Educational Psychologist, 32*(3), 137-151.

Beane, A. (1999). *The bully free classroom.* Minneapolis, MN: Free Spirit.

Benard, B. (1995). *Fostering resilience in children.* Urbana, IL: ERIC. (ERIC Document Reproduction No. EDO-PS-95-9)

Bennett, W. (1996). *The book of virtues: A treasury of great moral stories.* New York: Touchstone Books.

Benson, P., Galbraith, J., & Espeland, P. (1998). *What kids need to succeed.* Minneapolis, MN: Free Spirit.

Birch, S., & Ladd, G. (1997). The teacher-child relationship and children's early school adjustment. *Journal of School Psychology, 35*, 61-79.

Bluestein, J. (2001). *Creating emotionally safe schools: A guide for educators and parents.* Deerfield Beach, FL: Health Communications.

Bodine, R., & Crawford, D. (1999). *Developing emotional intelligence: Behavior management and conflict resolution in schools.* Champaign, IL: Research Press.

Bodine, R., Crawford, D., & Schrumpf, F. (1994). *Creating the peaceable school: A comprehensive program for teaching conflict resolution.* Champaign, IL: Research Press.

Bonds, M., & Stoker, S. (2000). *Bully-proofing your school: A comprehensive approach for middle schools.* Longmont, CO: Sopris West.

Brendtro, L., Brokenleg, M., & Van Bockern, S. (1998). *Reclaiming youth at risk: Our hope for the future.* Bloomington, IN: National Educational Service.

Brophy, J., & Good, T. (2000). *Looking in classrooms* (8th ed.). Boston: Allyn & Bacon.

Burns, T. (1996). *From risk to resilience.* Dallas, TX: Marco Polo.

Caine, R., & Caine, G. (1994). *Making connections: Teaching and the human brain.* Reading, MA: Addison-Wesley.

Center for Effective Collaboration and Practice. (1998). Addressing student problem behavior—An IEP team's introduction to functional behavioral assessment and behavior intervention plans (2nd ed.). Washington, DC: Federal Resource Center for Special Education.

Conduct Problems Prevention Research Group. (1999). Initial impact of the Fast Track prevention trial for conduct problems: I. The high-risk sample. *Journal of Consulting and Clinical Psychology, 67,* 631-647.

Corey, G. (2000). *Theory and practice of counseling and psychotherapy* (6th ed.). Pacific Grove, CA: Brooks/Cole.

Cummings, C. (2000). *Winning strategies for classroom management.* Alexandria, VA: Association for Supervision and Curriculum Development.

Curwin, R., & Mendler, A. (1999a). *Discipline with dignity.* Alexandria, VA: Association for Supervision and Curriculum Development.

Curwin, R., & Mendler, A. (1999b). *Discipline with dignity for challenging youth.* Bloomington, IN: National Educational Service.

Davis, M., Eshelman, E., & McKay, M. (2000). *The relaxation and stress reduction workbook.* Oakland, CA: New Harbinger.

Deschenes, C., Ebeling, D., & Sprague, J. (1994). *Adapting curriculum and instruction in inclusive classrooms: A teacher's desk reference.* Bloomington, IN: Institute for the Study of Developmental Disabilities.

DiGiulio, R. (2000). *Positive classroom management.* Thousand Oaks, CA: Corwin.

Doll, B. (1994). *Prevalence of psychiatric disorders in children and youth.* Manuscript submitted for publication.

Dwyer, K., Osher, D., & Warger, C. (1998). *Early warning, timely response: A guide to safe schools.* Washington, DC: U.S. Department of Education.

Elias, M. (1997). Reinterpreting dissemination of prevention programs as widespread implementation with effectiveness and fidelity. In R. P. Weissberg, T. P. Gullotta, et al. (Eds.), *Establishing preventive services* (Issues in Children's and Families' Lives, Vol. 9, pp. 253-289). Thousand Oaks, CA: Sage.

Elias, M., Zins, J., Weissberg, R., Frey, K., Greenberg, M., Haynes, N., et al. (1997). *Promoting social and emotional learning: Guidelines for educators.* Alexandria, VA: Association for Supervision and Curriculum Development.

Ellis, A., & Dryden, W. (1987). *The practice of rational emotive therapy.* New York: Springer.

Evertson, C., Emmer, E., & Worsham, M. (2003). *Classroom management for elementary teachers* (6th ed.). Boston: Allyn & Bacon.

Evertson, C., & Harris, A. (2003). *Classroom organization and management program (COMP): Creating conditions for learning.* Nashville, TN: Vanderbilt University.

Fay, J., & Funk, D. (1995). *Teaching with love and logic.* Golden, CO: Love and Logic Press.

Feindler, E. L., & Ecton, R. B. (1986). *Adolescent anger control: Cognitive-behavioral techniques.* Elmsford, NY: Pergamon Press.

Gettinger, M. (1988). Methods of proactive classroom management. *School Psychology Review, 17,* 227-242.

Gibbs, J. (1995). *Tribes: A new way of learning and being together.* Windsor, CA: CenterSource Systems.

Glasser, W. (1996). Unpublished lecture. Minneapolis, MN.

Glasser, W. (1998). *Choice theory: A new psychology of personal freedom.* New York: HarperCollins.

Glasser, W. (2000). *Every student can succeed.* San Diego: CA: Black Forest Press.

Glasser, W., & Glasser, C. (1999). *The language of choice theory.* New York: HarperCollins.

Glenn, S., & Nelsen, J. (1989). *Raising self-reliant children in a self-indulgent world.* Rocklin, CA: Prima.

Goldstein, A., Sprafkin, R., Gershaw, N., & Klein, P. (1980). *Skillstreaming the adolescent.* Champaign, IL: Research Press.

Goldstein, S. (1995). *Understanding and managing children's classroom behavior.* New York: John Wiley.

Goleman, D. (1995). *Emotional intelligence: Why it can matter more than IQ.* New York: Bantam Books.

Goleman, D. (1998). *Working with emotional intelligence.* New York: Bantam Books.

Gootman, M. (2001). *The caring teacher's guide to discipline: Helping young students learn self-control, responsibility, and respect.* Thousand Oaks, CA: Corwin.

Grotberg, E. (1995). *A guide to promoting resilience in children: Strengthening the human spirit.* The Hague, Netherlands: Bernard van Leer Foundation.

Hawkins, D., Doueck, H., & Lishner, D. (1988). Changing teaching practices in mainstreaming classroom to improve bonding and behavior of low achievers. *American Educational Research Journal, 25,* 31-50.

Hayes, C. (1987). *Risking the future: Adolescent sexuality, pregnancy, and child bearing* (Vol. 1). Washington, DC: National Academy Press.

Howes, C., Matheson, C., & Hamilton, C. (1994). Maternal, teacher, and child-care history correlates of children's relationships with peers. *Child Development, 65,* 264-273.

Hubble, M. A., Duncan, B. L., & Miller, S. D. (Eds.). (1999). *The heart and soul of change: What works in therapy.* Washington DC: American Psychological Association.

Jenkins, J., Pious, C., & Jewell, M. (1990). Special education and the regular education initiative: Basic assumptions. *Exceptional Children, 56,* 479-491.

Johnson, D., & Johnson, R. (1995). *Teaching students to be peacemakers.* Minneapolis, MN: Burgess.

Kagan, S. (1994). *Cooperative learning.* San Juan Capistrano, CA: Kagan Cooperative Learning.

Kendall, P. C., & Braswell, L. (1993). *Cognitive-behavioral therapy for impulsive children.* New York: Guilford Press.

Knoff, H. (2001). *The stop and think social skills program.* Longmont, CO: Sopris West.

Koegel, L. K., Koegel, R. L., & Dunlap, G. (1996). *Positive behavioral support: Including people with difficult behavior in the community.* Baltimore: Paul H. Brooks.

Kottler, J. (2002). *Students who drive you crazy: Succeeding with resistant, unmotivated, and otherwise difficult young people.* Thousand Oaks, CA: Corwin.

Krovetz, M. L. (1999). *Fostering resiliency: Expecting all students to use their minds and hearts well.* Thousand Oaks, CA: Corwin.

Kusche, C., & Greenberg, M. (1994). *The PATHS curriculum.* Seattle, WA: Developmental Research and Programs.

Lambert, M. (1992). Implications of outcome research for psychotherapy integration. In J. C. Norcross & M. R. Goldfried (Eds.), *Handbook of psychotherapy integration* (pp. 94-129). New York: Basic Books.

LaVigna, G. W., & Donellan, A. M. (1986). *Alternatives to punishment: Solving behavior problems with non-aversive strategies.* New York: Irvington.

LeDoux, J. (1998). *The emotional brain: The mysterious underpinnings of emotional life.* New York: Simon & Schuster.

Lochman, J., Dunn, S., & Klimes-Dougan, B. (1993). An intervention and consultation model from a social cognitive perspective: A description of the Anger Coping program. *School Psychology Review, 22*(3), 458-471.

Ludwig, S., & Mentley, K. (1997). *Quality is the key: Stories from the Huntington Woods School.* Wyoming, MI: KWM Educational Services.

Lynch, M., & Cicchetti, D. (1992). Maltreated children's reports of relatedness to their teachers. In R. C. Pianta (Ed.), *Relationships between children and non-parental adults* (New Directions in Child Development, Vol. 57, pp. 81-108). San Francisco: Jossey-Bass.

Lynch, M., & Cicchetti, D. (1997). Children's relationships with adults and peers: An examination of elementary and junior high school students. *Journal of Psychology, 35,* 81-100.

Marzano, R. J., Pickering, D. J., & Pollock, J. E. (2001). *Classroom instruction that works: Research-based strategies for increasing student achievement.* Alexandria, VA: Association for Supervision and Curriculum Development.

McCart, A., & Turnbull, A. (2002, October 31). The issues: Behavioral concerns. PBS Teachers Source: From the Start. Retrieved October, 2002, from http://www.pbs.org/teachersource/prek2/issues/402issue.shtm

McCaslin, M., & Good, T. (1998). Moving beyond the conception of management as sheer compliance: Helping students to develop goal coordination strategies. *Educational Horizons, 76*(4), 169-176.

McGinnis, E., & Goldstein, A. (1997). *Skillstreaming the elementary school child: New strategies and perspectives for teaching social skills.* Champaign, IL: Research Press.

Mendler, A. (2000). *Motivating students who don't care.* Bloomington, IN: National Educational Service.

Merrell, K. (2002). Social-emotional intervention in schools: Current status, progress, and promise. *Journal of School Psychology, 31,* 143-147.

MetLife Survey of the American Teacher. (2000). *The American teacher 2000: Are we preparing students for the 21st century?* New York: Author.

Michelson, L. (1987). Cognitive-behavioral strategies in the prevention and treatment of antisocial disorders in children and adolescents. In J. D. Burchard & S. N. Burchard (Eds.), *Prevention of delinquent behavior* (pp. 275-311). Newbury Park, CA: Sage.

Nelsen, J., Lott, L., & Glenn, S. (2000). *Positive discipline in the classroom: Developing mutual respect, cooperation, and responsibility in your classroom.* Roseville, CA: Prima.

Norton, B. (1995). *The quality classroom manager.* Amityville, NY: Baywood.

Olweus, D. (1999). *Bully prevention program.* Boulder, CO: Institute of Behavioral Science.

Pianta, R. (1997). Adult-child relationship processes and early schooling. *Early Education and Development, 8,* 11-26.

Pianta, R. (1999). *Enhancing relationships between children and teachers.* Washington, DC: American Psychological Association.

Rathvon, N. (1999). *Effective school interventions.* New York: Guilford Press.

Resnick, M., Bearman, P., Blum, R., Bauman, K., Harris, K., Jones, R., et al. (1997). Protecting adolescents from harm: Findings from the national longitudinal study on adolescent health. *Journal of the American Medical Association, 278,* 823-832.

Rogers, C., & Frieberg, H. J. (1994). *Freedom to learn* (3rd ed.). New York: Merrill.

Rutter, M. (1990). Psychosocial resilience and protective mechanisms. In J. Wolf, A. Masten, D. Cicchetti, K. H. Neuchterlein, & S. Weintraub (Eds.), *Risk and protective factors in the development of psychopathology* (pp. 102-127). New York: Cambridge University Press.

Ryan, A. M., Gheen, M., & Midgley, C. (1998). Why do some students avoid asking for help? An examination of the interplay among students' academic efficacy, teacher's social-emotional role and classroom goal structure. *Journal of Educational Psychology, 90,* 528-535.

Seligman, M. (1990). *Learned optimism.* New York: Simon & Schuster.

Seligman, M. (1995). *The optimistic child.* New York: Harper Perennial.

Shure, M. B. (2001). *An interpersonal cognitive problem-solving program: I can problem solve.* Champaign, IL: Research Press.

Skiba, R., & Peterson, R. (1999, January). The dark side of zero tolerance. *Phi Delta Kappan, 80,* 372-382.

Slavin, R. (1995). *Cooperative learning* (2nd ed.). Boston: Allyn & Bacon.

Solomon, D., Battistich, V., Kim, D., & Watson, M. (1997). Teacher practices associated with students' sense of the classroom as a community. *Social Psychology of Education, 1,* 235-267.

Sprick, R., Garrison, M., & Howard, L. (1998). *CHAMPs: A proactive and positive approach to classroom management.* Longmont, CO: Sopris West.

Thurlow, M., Christenson, S., Sinclair, M., Evelo, D., & Thornton, H. (1995). *Staying in school: Middle school students with learning and emotional disabilities* (ABD Dropout Prevention and Intervention Series, pp. 15-16). Minneapolis: Institute on Community Integration, University of Minnesota.

Tomlinson, C. (1999). *The differentiated classroom: Responding to the needs of all learners.* Alexandria, VA: Association for Supervision and Curriculum Development.

Tuma, J. (1989). Mental health services for children: The state of the art. *American Psychologist, 44,* 188-199.

U.S. Secret Service Safe School Initiative. (2000). *An interim report on the prevention of targeted school violence in schools.* Washington, DC: Author.

Walker, H., McConnell, S., Holmes, D., Todis, B., Walker, J., & Golden, N. (1983). *The Walker social skills curriculum: The ACCEPTS program.* Austin, TX: PRO-ED.

Walker, J., & Shea, T. (1991). *Behavior management: A practical approach for educators.* New York: Macmillan.

Wang, M., Elias, M., Walberg, H., Weissberg, R., & Zins, J. (2000). The other side of the report card. *CASEL Collections, 1,* 1-3.

Wang, M. C., Haertel, G. D., & Walberg, H. J. (1994). What helps students learn? *Educational Leadership, 51*(4), 74-79.

Werner, E., & Smith, R. (1989). *Vulnerable but invincible: A longitudinal study of resilient children and youth.* New York: Adams, Bannister, & Cox.

Wright, D. (1999). *Writing one page behavior plans that work: Behavior/discipline training.* Paper presented at a discipline training workshop, Boardman, OH.

Wubbolding, R. (1988). *Using reality therapy.* New York: Harper & Row.

Wubbolding, R. (1996). *Reality therapy training manual* (10th ed.). Cincinnati, OH: Center for Reality Therapy.

Wubbolding, R. (1999). *Cycle of managing, supervising, counseling, and coaching* (11th ed.). Cincinnati, OH: Center for Reality Therapy.

Wubbolding, R. (2000). *Reality therapy for the 21st century.* Philadelphia: Taylor & Francis.

Wubbolding, R., & Brickell, J. (2001). *A set of directions for putting and keeping yourself together.* Minneapolis, MN: Educational Media Corporation.

Ysseldyke, J. E., & Christenson, S. L. (1993). *The instructional environment system–II.* Longmont, CO: Sopris West.

Zins, J., Elias, M., Greenberg, M., & Kline Pruett, M. (2000). Issues in the implementation of prevention programs [Special issue]. *Journal of Educational and Psychological Consultation, 11*(1).

Zins, J., Elias, M., Weissberg, R., Greenberg, M., Haynes, N., Frey, K., et al. (1998). Enhancing learning through social and emotional education. *CASEL Collections, 2,* 1-3.

Index